COMMUNICATIONS
AND BROADCASTING

COMMUNICATIONS AND BROADCASTING

REVISED EDITION

FROM WIRED WORDS TO WIRELESS WEB

Harry Henderson

CHELSEA HOUSE
PUBLISHERS
An imprint of Infobase Publishing

Chelsea House
An imprint of Infobase Publishing
132 West 31st Street
New York NY 10001

Library of Congress Cataloging-in-Publication Data
Henderson, Harry.
   Communications and broadcasting : from wired words to wireless Web / Harry Henderson.—Rev. ed.
      p. cm.
   Includes bibliographical references and index.
   ISBN 0-8160-5748-6
   1. Telecommunication—History—Juvenile literature. I. Title.
   TK5102.4.H46 2006
   384—dc22
2006005577

Chelsea House books are available at special discounts when purchased in bulk quantities for businesses, associations, institutions, or sales promotions. Please call our Special Sales Department in New York at (212) 967-8800 or (800) 322-8755.

You can find Chelsea House on the World Wide Web at http://www.chelseahouse.com

Text design by James Scotto-Lavino
Cover design by Dorothy M. Preston
Illustrations by Sholto Ainslie and Melissa Ericksen

Printed in the United States of America
MP FOF 10 9 8 7 6 5 4 3 2 1

This book is printed on acid-free paper.

To my fellow dwellers in The WELL,
for 20 years of exploring virtual community

CONTENTS

PREFACE

The Milestones in Science and Discovery set is based on a simple but powerful idea—that science and technology are not separate from people's daily lives. Rather, they are part of seeking to understand and reshape the world, an activity that virtually defines being human.

More than a million years ago, the ancestors of modern humans began to shape stones into tools that helped them compete with the specialized predators around them. Starting about 35,000 years ago, the modern type of human, *Homo sapiens,* also created elaborate cave paintings and finely crafted art objects, showing that technology had been joined with imagination and language to compose a new and vibrant world of culture. Humans were not only shaping their world but also representing it in art and thinking about its nature and meaning.

Technology is a basic part of that culture. The mythologies of many peoples include a "trickster" figure who upsets the settled order of things and brings forth new creative and destructive possibilities. In many myths, for instance, a trickster such as the Native Americans' Coyote or Raven steals fire from the gods and gives it to human beings. All technology, whether it harnesses fire, electricity, or the energy locked in the heart of atoms or genes, partakes of the double-edged gift of the trickster, providing power to both hurt and heal.

An inventor of technology is often inspired by the discoveries of scientists. Science as we know it today is younger than technology, dating back about 500 years to a period called the Renaissance. During the Renaissance, artists and thinkers began to explore nature systematically, and the first modern scientists, such as Leonardo da Vinci (1452–1519) and Galileo Galilei (1564–1642), used instruments and experiments to develop and test ideas about how objects in the universe behaved. A succession of revolutions followed, often introduced by individual geniuses: Isaac Newton (1643–1727) in mechanics and mathematics, Charles Darwin (1809–82) in biological evolution, Albert Einstein (1879–1955) in relativity and quantum physics, and James Watson (1928–) and Francis Crick (1916–2004) in modern genetics. Today's emerging fields of science and technology, such as genetic engineering, nanotechnology, and artificial intelligence, have their own inspiring leaders.

The fact that particular names such as Newton, Darwin, and Einstein can be so easily associated with these revolutions suggests the importance of the individual in modern science and technology. Each book in this series thus focuses on the lives and achievements of eight to 10 individuals who together have revolutionized an aspect of science or technology. Each book presents a different field: marine science, genetics, astronomy and space science, forensic science, communications technology, robotics, artificial intelligence, and mathematical simulation. Although early pioneers are included where appropriate, the emphasis is generally on researchers who worked in the 20th century or are still working today.

While the biographies in each volume are placed in an order that reflects the flow of the individuals' major achievements, these life stories are often intertwined. The achievements of particular men and women cannot be understood without some knowledge of the times in which they lived, the people with whom they worked, and the developments that preceded their research. Newton famously remarked, "if I have seen further [than others], it is by standing on the shoulders of giants." Each scientist or inventor builds upon—or wrestles with—the work that has come before. Individual scientists and inventors also interact with others in their own laboratories and elsewhere, sometimes even partaking in vast collective efforts, such as when U.S. government and private projects raced, at the end of the 20th century, to complete the description of the human genome. Scientists and inventors affect, and are affected by, economic, political, and social forces as well. The relationship between scientific and technical creativity and developments in social institutions is another important facet of this set.

A number of additional features provide further context for the biographies in these books. Each chapter includes a chronology and suggestions for further reading. In addition, a glossary and a general bibliography (including organizations and Web resources) appear at the end of each book. Several types of sidebars are also used in the text to explore particular aspects of the profiled scientists' and inventors' work:

Connections   Describes the relationship between the featured work and other scientific or technical developments

I Was There   Presents firsthand accounts of discoveries or inventions

Issues   Discusses scientific or ethical issues raised by the discovery or invention

Other Scientists (or Inventors)   Describes other individuals who played an important part in the work being discussed

Parallels   Shows parallel or related discoveries

Social Impact   Suggests how the discovery or invention affects or might affect society and daily life

Solving Problems   Explains how a scientist or inventor dealt with a particular technical problem or challenge

Trends   Presents data or statistics showing how developments in a field changed over time

The hope is that readers will be intrigued and inspired by these stories of the human quest for understanding, exploration, and innovation.

ACKNOWLEDGMENTS

I wish to express my appreciation to my editor, Frank K. Darmstadt, for his ongoing help in keeping this project on track, and to the copy editor, Amy L. Conver, for her skillfull handling of this manuscript. I also want to thank my wife, Lisa Yount, for helping keep track of matters of format and style as she completed her own volumes in the Milestones set.

INTRODUCTION

In the past two centuries, two webs have grown to cover the Earth: a web of connectivity and a web of information. The revolution in communications and broadcasting is about how inventors, scientists, and entrepreneurs have created technologies that have transformed the way humans communicate, obtain news, look up information, conduct business, seek entertainment, and form communities.

A Growing Web

Imagine you are a Martian who has been observing the Earth with powerful instruments for the past 160 years or so. When you first began watching, around the year 1840 (Earth time), you saw wires on poles starting to spread across the North American and European continents, carrying signals that went "dit-dat-dit." About 1860 Earth time, you might have noticed ships unreeling thick wire cables down to the ocean floor, crossing from one continent to another. About 1880, your sensitive instruments might have been able to tell that some wires now carried the sounds of speech.

By 1900, you started to pick up electromagnetic signals that traveled through space without wires. Around 1920, the Earth's atmosphere started to fill with broadcasts of speech and music. By 1930, crude pictures were also beaming out into space: Television had been born.

As the 20th century progressed, you saw that what had been separate networks of wires and radio signals had begun to merge into a thick, pulsing web of information. The information shuttled from place to place far too quickly to be controlled by a living hand. Invented at mid-century, the digital computer had come of age by the millennium, merging formerly separate media and profoundly changing the way humans learned about their world, traded goods and services, and forged social connections.

Reinventing the Inventor

This volume in the Milestones in Discovery and Invention set is about the inventors and inventions that made modern communications and broadcasting possible and repeatedly transformed its media. The story has several interwoven threads.

First, there is the development and interconnection of scientific ideas: electromagnetism leading to the telegraph and telephone; Maxwell's wave theory leading to radio and television; communications and information theory from Claude Shannon leading to the World Wide Web and beyond.

Then there are the inventors themselves: the people who visualized how scientific ideas could be applied to create new communications and information devices. Inventors had to be part scientist, part engineer, and part business entrepreneur. It was not enough to have an idea: Inventors had to be able to convince people that their inventions were useful and worth investing in.

Changing Roles

Another theme of these stories of discovery is how a changing society has viewed inventions and inventors. Each of the inventions and ideas discussed in this book have had profound social effects that went beyond helping people communicate or become informed or entertained. The telephone, for example, gave women more social freedom and also brought many of them into the workplace. The phonograph largely changed music from something to be made together at home to a product people could buy. Movies and television brought powerful images that a whole nation might share. The World Wide Web created by Tim Berners-Lee now draws together every form of media and carries a growing portion of the world's commerce.

The same society that was changed by inventions also changed the role of the inventor. Nineteenth-century America created and celebrated the inventor-hero who single-handedly turned an idea into an industry. By the mid-20th century, however, invention had become a product produced in giant corporate laboratories. While Thomas Edison and Guglielmo Marconi had created mighty companies and shaped the growth of industries, radio pioneer Edwin Armstrong and television wizard Philo Farnsworth found their ideas largely held hostage by the needs of the giant RCA Corporation. Yet starting in the 1970s, computer and networking pioneers working in garage laboratories and even college dorms again reshaped the communication industry.

Transforming Media

This book features four types of invention: communication, media, broadcasting, and the convergence of all three with information technology in the digital age. The chapters on Samuel Morse, Alexander Graham Bell, and Guglielmo Marconi deal with point-to-point communications: the wired and wireless telegraph and the telephone. The chapter on Thomas Edison focuses on his two great media inventions: sound recording (the phonograph) and the motion picture.

The chapters devoted to Edwin Armstrong and Philo Farnsworth feature the inventions that made broadcast media (radio and television) possible. The stories of these two inventors also mark the rise of corporate media power and the struggle of the individual inventor to retain control over his or her invention.

The Digital Convergence

The final four chapters mark the rise of the digital age and the ways in which communication, media, and information have converged. Claude Shannon developed the information theory that made modern digital media and data storage possible, while exploring the possibilities of the digital computer as a tool of intelligence.

J. C. R. Licklider used his background in psychology and neuroscience to develop new ways for people and computers to interact, and he also envisioned and guided the development of what would become the Internet. Tim Berners-Lee used that platform to link together information through the World Wide Web. Finally, writer Howard Rheingold explored new forms of community made possible by online computer systems and mobile communications technology.

This story is continuing, with new chapters being written every day. Young people keep in constant touch through text messaging. Cell phone users beam pictures of office parties—but can also capture natural disasters and riots. Elaborate virtual worlds have gained the allegiance and waking hours of legions of online gamers. While no one truly knows what might happen next, considering the inventors and inventions of the past can reveal patterns of change and development that can help people prepare for the future.

1

WRITING WITH LIGHTNING

SAMUEL MORSE AND THE ELECTROMAGNETIC TELEGRAPH

On January 27, 2006, many newspaper readers were no doubt bemused to read a story about Western Union's announcement that it was ending its telegraph service. Most people who are not old enough to receive Social Security have never sent or received a telegram. In fact, Western Union has not actually used a telegraph for decades: Its messages instead have traveled over phone lines and have mainly involved money transfers.

It is hard to imagine, but a century and a half ago, news could spread only as fast as a stagecoach or ship could travel. This changed when an artist and part-time inventor named Samuel Morse decided that he could harness a mysterious force called electricity to carry messages in a wire.

Samuel Morse used the principle of electromagnetism to create the first practical telegraph system. (Library of Congress)

1

Samuel Finley Breese Morse (1791–1872) was born in Charleston, Massachusetts. The son of a Calvinist minister, Morse received a liberal education in both science and the arts at Yale College (later called Yale University). He became a skillful painter and the first president of the National Academy of Design.

Inventing the Inventor

Like many artists throughout history, however, Morse discovered that it was hard to make a living from his art. By 1837, Morse had decided embark on a new career as an inventor. People had been inventing things for thousands of years, but the idea of inventing as a profession was something new—but something that greatly appealed to people in the young United States. In his book *InfoCulture,* Steven Lubar notes that "Americans celebrated the 'ingenious Yankee,' praised his cleverness at machines, and admired his ability to 'get things done.' That a project was technologically challenging was in itself a reason to do it."

By the early 19th century, Americans seemed to be confident that they could solve any technical problem. They also felt an increasing need for inventions that would help them manage a nation that was rapidly expanding in size and population. By the 1830s, the United States had grown to 24 states with a total population of about 13 million people. A generation earlier, in 1803, the Louisiana Purchase had extended the young nation all the way to the Rocky Mountains. Two inventions, the steamboat and the railroad, were beginning to form a transportation network that linked cities such as New York and Philadelphia with new western communities such as St. Louis, Missouri, and Cincinnati, Ohio.

The Need for Communications

Even as transportation was improving, communications remained difficult. Mail could be carried by stagecoach or by a post rider on horseback between eastern cities such as New York and Philadelphia in only a day or so. Messages to interior cities such as Chicago or

Cincinnati could take weeks, however. In 1837, the United States Senate asked for proposals for a nationwide telegraph system that could send important messages without delay.

The word *telegraph* comes from the Greek words *tele,* meaning "far," and *graphein,* "to write." At the time, *telegraph* meant a visual system for relaying signals from point to point. Typically, a series of towers called semaphores used movable arms that displayed combinations of flags. The crew of each tower had a spotter who used a telescope to read the message from an adjacent tower. A flag crew then relayed, or repeated, the message so the next tower down the line could see it. Semaphore systems could be quite extensive: In France, chains of semaphore stations had linked the cities of Paris and Lille by the 1790s. Unfortunately, semaphore systems needed a tower and crew every five to 10 miles (8 to 16 km), and each repetition of a message took time and introduced the possibility of error. Thus, semaphore systems were generally limited to sending brief messages.

The Electric Alternative

In 1832, as his ship was returning to New York City from an art study trip to Europe, Morse thought of a different way to send messages. He had read about Benjamin Franklin's pioneering electrical experiments nearly a century earlier, and, ever since, Morse had been fascinated by the mysterious power of electricity. Dr. Charles T. Jackson, a fellow passenger, remarked one day that electricity passes instantaneously through any length of wire. According to Lewis Coe's history of the telegraph, Morse excitedly replied that "If this be so, and the presence of electricity can be made visible in any desired part of the circuit, I see no reason why intelligence [information] might not be instantaneously transmitted by electricity to any distance."

Morse was not the first person to arrive at this insight. In 1816, English inventor Francis Ronalds had sent messages using charges of static electricity. This form of electricity is generated by friction, usually from a turning wheel. The electricity is discharged in very brief bursts that are hard to detect or manipulate.

In 1800, however, the Italian scientist Alessandro Volta had invented a device that generated a continuous flow, or current, of electricity. It used a group, or "battery," of disks of zinc and silver, separated by felt disks soaked in a salty solution of brine. This kind of electricity proved much easier to control and use.

In order to use electricity for carrying signals, there had to be a receiver—something that could detect the electrical pulses at the other end of the circuit. In 1819, Danish professor Hans Christian Ørsted discovered that when electricity was sent through a wire, it made a nearby compass needle move. Ørsted had discovered electromagnetism, the idea that electricity and magnetism were interchangeable forms of energy. Other experimenters discovered how to wind wire around a piece of metal to make a powerful magnet. Since the magnetism occurred only while electricity flowed, it could be used to move a needle or switch each time an electrical pulse was received.

Once they had a battery, a switch, and an electromagnet for detecting current, many experimenters realized that they could use an electrical current to carry messages. Most of them, however, were more interested in developing a theory to explain electromagnetism than in building practical devices that used it. Most scientists of the early 19th century did not often think about what is today called "technology"—they left that to people who were dismissed as "mechanics" or "tinkerers."

Morse's First Telegraph

In 1837, when Morse had decided to be an inventor, he reviewed his 1832 notebooks. He had to translate his ideas into a practical device. Two things caused him considerable difficulty. First, while he had read about electricity, Morse was not a scientist. Knowing he had to learn more about electrical theory, he asked Dr. Leonard Gale, a geologist, for help. Gale soon became Morse's partner in the telegraph project, and, in turn, he put Morse in touch with Joseph Henry, a pioneering researcher in electromagnetism. Henry noted that Morse had "very little knowledge of the general principles of electricity, magnetism, or electro-magnetism." While Henry thought that his own work gave him a better claim to a telegraph patent than Morse, he also felt that scientists should not get patents. (Later, when Morse's telegraph became successful, Henry came to regret his decision.)

Morse's other big problem was that he was not a particularly good mechanic or engineer. He did, however, have the useful ability to improvise from materials at hand. Because his brother was a printer, Morse had some familiarity with the tools of that trade. For his telegraph transmitter, Morse cast lead type so that it had groups of raised ridges. Each group represented a number. He built a mechanism by which a stick passed over each ridge, briefly dipping wires into cups of mercury, which conducted electricity, then closing the circuit to a battery and sending an electrical pulse. For example, to send the number three, there would be three ridges to send three pulses.

The telegraph receiver was built on a canvas-stretching frame from Morse's art studio. On it, he mounted an electromagnet that pulled an arm holding a pencil. Under the pencil, a clockwork mechanism pulled a strip of paper. Each time an electrical impulse

---

OTHER INVENTORS: THE WHEATSTONE TELEGRAPH

There are many possible ways in which information can be signaled and received in an electrical circuit. While Samuel Morse was working on the telegraph in the United States, English inventors William Fothergill Cooke (1806–79) and Charles Wheatstone (1802–75) patented a different type of telegraph.

The Wheatstone telegraph used five wires and five needles. Each needle could point two different ways, depending on the direction of a current sent to it. By triggering combinations of needles, the telegraph could point to one of 25 letters of the alphabet printed on a board underneath the needles. While these letters could be read without knowing any special codes, it was much more expensive to run a telegraph line with five wires instead of only one. The English inventors later modified their telegraph to use a single wire and a code similar to that of Morse's system.

was received, the electromagnet pulled the arm and pencil, making a V-shaped mark on the moving paper.

To read the message, the operator counted the marks to see what number each group represented. Each three digits were looked up in a code book. For example, the digits *215* stood for the word *successful*.

Improving the Telegraph

Morse's first telegraph worked, and after Gale showed him how to make a more powerful electromagnet by winding more turns of wire, Morse was able to send a message 10 miles.

Unfortunately, the device was complicated and subject to frequent breakdowns. One day, Alfred Vail, who had been a student

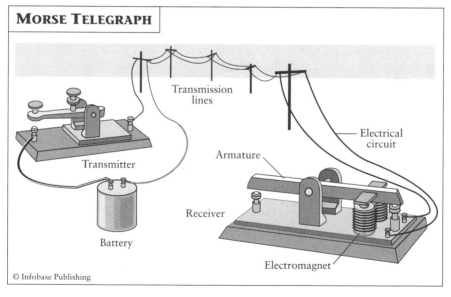

MORSE TELEGRAPH

© Infobase Publishing

The Morse telegraph sends an electrical signal by using a switch or key to momentarily complete a circuit with a battery. At the receiver, the surge of current causes magnetism, which in turn moves an arm, making a click or triggering a printing mechanism.

at New York University as well as a skilled mechanic, saw Morse's telegraph. Vail became enthusiastic about the project. In exchange for a quarter share of future profits, Vail agreed to build an improved telegraph.

Morse obtained a patent for the telegraph in 1840. He hoped that the federal government would buy his patent and set up a nation-wide telegraph system. Morse felt that the telegraph, like the postal system, canals, and national roads, was a benefit to all Americans. The Senate, after all, had asked for a semaphore system, and Morse was ready to provide something much better. As recounted in Steven Lubar's book *InfoCulture,* Morse believed that if the government did not buy the telegraph, it would be controlled by "a company of speculators," and it would become "a means of enriching the corporation at the expense of the bankruptcy of thousands."

In March 1843, Congress finally agreed to appropriate $30,000 for Morse and Vail to build a telegraph line from Washington, D.C., to Baltimore, Maryland, as a demonstration. Morse and Vail soon realized that the first model of the telegraph was too complicated and unreliable for regular service. They made two major improvements. They replaced the slug of type and mercury switch with a simple spring-loaded key to open and close the circuit. Instead of using numbers to stand for words, they represented each letter or numeral with a pattern of short pulses (transcribed as dots) and long pulses (represented by dashes). For example, the letter E was a single dot, and the letter X was a dot, a dash, and two more dots. This system became known as Morse code.

The telegraph line was completed in 1844. The first official message Morse sent was "What hath God wrought [done]?" That year, a presidential election took place, and the telegraph was used to relay news from the Democratic and Whig party conventions.

Despite this success, Congress showed little interest in setting up a government-run telegraph system. After the first flurry of messages, people seemed to have trouble finding a use for the invention. As author Steven Lubar points out, "Businesses weren't set up for dealing with telegraph messages. For a new technology to be successful, customers have to be told that they need it, and shown how to use it, and how to reorganize their operations around it. They have to convince themselves of its value."

Early telegraph lines also continued to suffer from unreliability. The telegraph was the first major electrical technology to be developed. This meant that engineers and technicians had to learn all the basic rules for dealing with electricity safely and avoiding short circuits. One telegraph builder admitted that "insulation was a long word that few of us understood."

Wiring the Nation

Gradually, businesspeople did begin to see how getting news before their competitors could be profitable. The investor who first learned about changes in stock or commodity prices could buy or sell favorably. The nation's growing entanglements in the world also demanded a better way to transmit information. During the Mexican War in 1846, newspapers and their readers realized that a telegraph could have brought them news in hours instead of days and weeks.

By 1847, telegraph lines stretched down the east coast of the United States from New York City to New Orleans, Louisiana, and by 1854, there were 30,000 miles (48,000 km) of telegraph wire around the country. As quoted by Stephen Lubar, Samuel Bowles, editor of the *Springfield Republican,* wrote in 1851 that

> *The increase of facilities for the transmission of news brought in a new era. The railroad car, the steamboat, and the magnetic telegraph have made neighborhood among widely dissevered [separated] States . . . These active and almost miraculous agencies have brought the whole civilized world in contact.*

Not everyone hailed this mid-century technological revolution. In his famous book *Walden,* Henry David Thoreau made a complaint that sounds quite familiar to modern television news viewers:

> *We are in great haste to construct a magnetic telegraph from Maine to Texas; but Maine and Texas, it may be, have nothing important to communicate . . . We are eager to tunnel under the Atlantic and bring*

the Old World some weeks nearer to the New; but perchance the first
news that will leak through into the broad, flapping American ear will
be that Princess Adelaide has the whooping cough.

Wizards of the Wires

Early telegraph operators had something like the status of today's top computer programmers. They could work for a few months at high wages and move on to another good job when they became bored. Telegraphers found more efficient ways to work. They soon learned that they could write down messages by listening to the pattern of clicks on the line, rather than waiting for them to be printed out. A simple "sounder" replaced complicated printing mechanisms.

PARALLELS: ROUTING MESSAGES

The telegraph system was actually made of many separate lines linking major cities, plus smaller lines that connected cities to outlying towns. Suppose one wanted to send a message from Philadelphia, Pennsylvania, to Frederick, Maryland. The telegrapher in Philadelphia sends the message along the Philadelphia–Washington, D.C., line with a header that says something like "To Baltimore, relay to Frederick." Most of the operators on the line would ignore the message as soon as they heard the "Baltimore" part. The Baltimore operator, however, would copy down the message and resend it to Frederick.

The modern Internet uses the same principle for sending information around the world. When a user sends an e-mail message, for example, the local computer breaks it up into a number of "packets" of data. Each packet has a header that includes the destination address as well as noting the packet's sequence within the whole message. Instead of human telegraphers, the computer network uses machines called routers to find the most efficient route for forwarding each packet. At the destination mail server, the packets are sorted back into order and assembled into complete messages.

Experienced operators could even sleep through the night shift and ignore the machine's clattering, confident that they would awaken instantly for any message beginning with their station's address.

The Telegraph at War

As with later technologies such as television and the Internet, telegraph enthusiasts tended to look toward a technological utopia. Gordon Bennett, editor of the *New York Herald,* is quoted by Lubar as believing that the telegraph could "do more to guard

As *shown in this engraving, during the Civil War, spies tapped enemy telegraph lines.* (Smithsonian Institution Photo No. 89-21052)

against disunion . . . then all the most experienced, the most saga-
cious [wise], and the most patriotic government could accomplish."

But improvements in communication could not address such facts
as Georgia and New York having very different opinions on slavery
and trade issues. When the Civil War broke out in 1861, both sides
began to realize that technology had become an important part of
the war effort. Railroads could move troops and supplies into battle
at unprecedented speeds. The telegraph made it possible to coordi-
nate military operations across hundreds of miles. By the end of the
war in 1865, the Union had built 15,000 miles (24,000 km) of military telegraph line and handled more than 6 million messages. The
Confederates, who trailed the North in technology and resources,
built only 1,000 miles (1600 km) and relied mainly on existing commercial lines.

Fast-moving groups of cavalry raiders attacked the enemy's railroads and the telegraph lines that often ran alongside them. Scouts
with portable telegraph sets soon began tapping into the enemy's
wires and eavesdropping on their messages. This, in turn, promoted
the development of codes and ciphers to protect the most important
messages.

Spanning the Globe

By the 1860s, the United States had leapfrogged the continent all the
way to the west coast. The gold rush of 1849 and its aftermath had
brought a need to link the growing population of California with
the rest of the Union.

In 1860, Congress authorized contracts for completing a telegraph
across the nation; work began in May 1861. The effort would be
hampered by many difficulties. Since there was no transcontinental
railroad yet, workers had to travel by wagon train. Wires and insula-
tors for the western part of the line had to be shipped around Cape
Horn at the tip of South America. On the plains, buffalo rubbed
their itching backs against the poles and knocked them over. Some
Native Americans admired the "magic" in the wires, but others
attacked what they saw as yet another intrusion by the white man
into their lands. Lightning storms could easily knock out part of

the line. Despite all these obstacles, the line was completed that October, well ahead of schedule.

As the United States became more industrialized, it needed to keep in touch with overseas markets for manufactured goods. America's most important trading partner, Great Britain, had even more need for overseas communications because it administered a worldwide empire "on which the sun never set." By the 1850s, engineers had begun to lay underwater telegraph lines for short distances. In 1858, Cyrus Field succeeded in getting investors in both the United States and Britain to finance a project to build a telegraph line from New York City to London. The cable ran northeast to Newfoundland and then followed a route via Greenland, Iceland, and the Orkney Islands that had been charted by depth soundings from naval ships.

Laying the transatlantic cable pushed telegraph technology to its limits. The cable had to be carefully insulated against the salty ocean. It was easy for the cable to become snarled as it was fed from huge drums over the side of a steamship on the tossing sea. The first attempt failed when the cable broke after four days. In August 4, 1858, however, the crew succeeded in running out the full length of cable. Unfortunately, operators in New York and London could barely hear the test messages, and after a few weeks, the cable failed completely. Later, the engineers realized that a spool of cable had been left out in the hot sun after it had been manufactured. The insulation had probably melted off, so that the cable short-circuited and discharged into the ground once it was in the ocean. In 1865, Field chartered the *Great Eastern,* the world's largest steamship, to lay a new cable. That cable was also lost, but a third try was successful.

The Atlantic cable expedition evoked feelings not unlike the exploration of space a hundred years later. As quoted by Arthur C. Clarke, Henry Field reported the first day aboard the *Niagara* during the 1858 transatlantic cable attempt:

Slow passed the hours of that day. But all went well, and the ships were moving out into the broad Atlantic. At length the sun went down in the west and stars came out on the face of the deep. But no man slept. A thousand eyes were watching a great experiment as [though

---

SOLVING PROBLEMS: LONG-DISTANCE TELEGRAPHY

Sending telegraph messages over long distances was difficult because electrical resistance in the wires weakened the signal as it traveled through the miles of wire. Having a telegraph station and operator every few miles was expensive. An invention called the relay helped solve this problem. The relay was simply an electromagnetic switch that responded to each signal by closing a circuit to a battery and sending a new copy of the signal down the line to the next section.

The transoceanic cables brought a new problem. Electrical scientist Michael Faraday calculated that the very long line would act as a capacitor (a device that stores an electric charge). This makes it take longer for a signal to build up to the level at which it could be detected at the other end of the line. Relays could not be used to solve this problem, because the line was thousands of feet under the ocean. Instead, engineers came up with extremely sensitive detectors that could respond to very faint signals. One such detector was so sensitive that it easily picked up a signal sent from the other side of the ocean, using no more power than that of a modern watch battery.

---

having] a personal interest in the issue . . . There was a strange, unnatural silence in the ship. Men paced the deck with a soft and muffled tread, speaking only in whispers, as if a loud voice or a heavy footfall might snap the vital cord. So much have they grown to feel for the enterprise, that the cable seemed to them like a human creature, on whose fate they hung, as if it were to decide their own destiny ...

The Telegraph Goes Corporate

The expanding telegraph business of the 1860s attracted investors who created new corporations. One of these, Western Union, bought out its main competitors in 1866. This single company then controlled 37,380 miles (59,800 km) of line with 2,250 offices. The monopoly did improve service, by standardizing equipment and procedures. On the other hand, workers lost much of their bargaining power, and the telegrapher went from being a skilled technician to little more than a clerk. Many women were hired into the field because they could be paid lower wages.

By the 1870s, the telegraph had become an indispensable part of American life. In an 1873 article, *Harper's Magazine* featured the telegraph and its many uses:

> *The fluctuation in the markets; the price of stocks; the premium on gold; the starting of railroad trains; the sailing of ships; the arrival of passengers; orders for merchandise and manufacturers of every kind; bargains offered and bargains closed; sermons, lectures, and political speeches; fires; sickness and death; weather reports; the approach of the grasshopper and the weevil; the transmission of money; the congratulation of friends—everything, from the announcement of a new planet down to the inquiry for a lost carpetbag, has its turn passing the wires.*

Morse, meanwhile, had profited by his dedication to the telegraph. He had enjoyed a comfortable estate and a happy family life. When he died in 1872, the news was quickly spread by the clattering telegraph keys.

Morse was a prototype for later American innovators in technology. Using his imagination and business skill, he had taken ideas from the frontiers of science, built a device that fulfilled emerging human needs, and convinced people to create a new industry.

Expansion and Decline

By the late 19th century, American cities were being crisscrossed by a maze of telegraph wires. As the message traffic increased, engineers sought an alternative to stringing still more wire. There were two basic ways to increase the capacity of the telegraph system.

The first way was to speed up the sending of messages so that each line could carry more traffic. On some systems, messages were keyed onto a punched tape on a special typewriter and then sent at high speed through an automatic transmitter. At the other end, a printing receiver "typed" out the messages faster than the most skilled of the old telegraphers could do.

The second approach was to make it possible to send more than one message at a time. In 1874, Thomas Edison built a "quadraplex" telegraph that could send two messages from each end of the line. In 1876, rival inventors Alexander Graham Bell and Elisha Gray invented a "harmonic telegraph." This instrument sent several messages at once. Each message had pulses that vibrated at a different frequency. Only the receiver for the proper frequency responded to each message. An assortment of techniques were thus available to cope with the 32 million telegraph messages that traveled through the nation's 12,000 telegraph offices in 1880.

By the early 20th century, the telegraph was a mature technology. A rival, the telephone, began to replace it for many uses (see chapter 2, "Voices in the Wires.") The telephone allowed people to talk in their own voices without operators or codes. Another technology, the teletype, let operators type messages and send them along telephone lines. As the century progressed, these technologies were joined by the facsimile (fax) machine and computer networks. Today the telegraph has been almost forgotten.

While the telegraph has vanished from today's world, it has left traces behind. Whenever someone sends money by Western Union or sends "flowers by wire" to a sweetheart, he or she is using services that originally operated by telegraph.

The most important legacy of the telegraph, though, is that it first taught people how to package information and send it at the speed of light by means of electricity. It changed the pace of business and daily life and gave news from distant places a new kind of immediacy. Linking cities and factories of the industrial world, the telegraph was the world's first "information superhighway."

Chronology

1791	Samuel F. B. Morse is born in Charleston, Massachusetts
1819	Danish professor Hans Christian Ørsted discovers electromagnetism

1832	While returning from studying art in Europe, Morse conceives the idea for an electromagnetic telegraph
1837	Resolved to make his living as an inventor, Morse seeks technical and business help for the invention. A simplified key-based telegraph is developed
1838	Morse sends the first message using the new alphabetic "Morse code"
1840	Morse patents his first telegraph system
1844	"What hath God wrought?" is sent on the first regular telegraph line, from Washington, D.C., to Baltimore
1850	Skilled telegraph operators learn to receive messages by ear rather than printing them
1854	The United States now has 30,000 miles (48,000 km) of telegraph line
1858	Cyrus Field's first attempt at a transatlantic telegraph fails
1860	Automatic repeaters extend the range of telegraph land lines by hundreds of miles
1861	The transcontinental telegraph is completed; the telegraph is used for military messages and spying during the Civil War
1866	The first successful transatlantic telegraph line is completed
1872	Morse dies after receiving many honors
1874–76	Thomas Edison, Alexander Graham Bell, and Elisha Gray invent telegraphs that can send multiple messages at the same time
1930	Associated Press closes its last telegraph line
2006	On January 27, Western Union officially discontinues telegraph service (which had not used actual telegraphs for many years)

Further Reading

Books

Clarke, Arthur C. *How the World Was One: Beyond the Global Village*. New York: Bantam Books, 1992.
  A famous science-fiction and fact writer offers an engaging account of how communications technology changed the world.
Coe, Lewis. *The Telegraph: A History of Morse's Invention and Its Predecessors in the United States*. Jefferson, N.C.: McFarland & Company, 1993.
  Describes the development of the telegraph in the United States and its use in daily life.
Latham, Jean L. *Samuel F. B. Morse*. Broomall, Pa.: Chelsea House Publishers, 1991.
  Biography of Morse for young readers.
Lubar, Stephen. *InfoCulture: The Smithsonian Book of Information Age Inventions*. Boston: Houghton Mifflin, 1993.
  Includes an account of the development of the telegraph and related inventions.
Standage, Tom. *The Victorian Internet: The Remarkable Story of the Telegraph and the Nineteenth Century's Online Pioneers*. New York: Walker and Company, 1998.
  Describes how a rapidly growing technology inspired idealism and created a culture of skilled technicians who chatted across their own online network more than a century before the Internet.
Tiner, John H. *Samuel F. B. Morse: Artist with a Message*. Milford, Conn.: Mott Media, 1987.
  Biography of Morse as inventor and artist; for younger readers.

Web Sites

Bellis, Mary. "The History of the Telegraph and Telegraphy." About. com. URL: http://inventors.about.com/library/inventors/bltele graph.htm. Accessed on August 28, 2006.
  Includes information about Morse, a time line, and links to illustrations such as the original patent drawings for the telegraph.
Smithsonian Institution. National Museum of American History. "Information Age: People, Information & Technology." Available

online. URL: http://photo2.si.edu/infoage/infoage.html. Accessed on December 27, 2005.

Includes a series of historical photos chronicling the development of communications and information technology from the telegraph to early computers.

"Telegraph Lore." Available online. URL: http://www.faradic.net/~gsraven/index.shtml#contents. Accessed on February 6, 2006.

A fan of telegraph history and lore has assembled a rich collection of pictures, guides to books and museums, and amusing anecdotes.

2
VOICES ON THE WIRES

ALEXANDER GRAHAM BELL AND THE TELEPHONE

A little more than a 100 years ago, talking with people meant meeting with them. With mail or even the telegraph, people could exchange messages but not carry on a true conversation. The telephone changed all of that.

Today the telephone is ubiquitous—in the form of the cell phone, it has even become a combination fashion accessory and extra appendage. The phone has probably done more than any other technology to change the way people interact and the way society is organized. Oddly enough, it all began because Alexander Graham Bell wanted to help deaf people learn to speak.

Sound and Silence

Alexander Graham Bell was born in 1847 in Edinburgh, Scotland. His father, Alexander Melville Bell, was a speech teacher. In 1864, the elder Bell worked out a system called Visible Speech. It used symbols to represent all the sounds that people make when speaking. He hoped to use his "sound alphabet" to teach deaf people how to speak. Many deaf people have trouble speaking clearly because they cannot hear what they are saying. With Visible Speech, they could practice making individual sounds and then put them together to form words.

Young Alexander (or "Aleck") Bell was fascinated by his father's work. He helped his father demonstrate Visible Speech to

Alexander Graham Bell was interested in helping the deaf, so he studied the transmission of sound. The result was the telephone. (Library of Congress)

visiting scientists. When he was 16, Bell's father challenged him and his older brother, Melville, to design a machine that could make speech sounds. The boys studied the larynx, or voice box, from a lamb. They built a model voice box that made different sounds when moved with levers while air blew through it.

While still a teenager, Bell became a schoolteacher. In his spare time, he studied how the mouth changes shape while making vowel sounds. Using tuning forks, he discovered that each sound is made up of a combination of tones. He later learned that a German physicist named Herman von Helmholtz had already done this work—and furthermore, that he had used electrically operated tuning forks to reproduce the sounds! In *The Making of the Electrical Age,* Harold I. Sharlin quotes Bell as noting that

[t]he interview had the effect of arousing my interest in the subjects of sound and electricity, and I did not rest until I had obtained possession of a copy of Helmholz's great work, and had attempted, in a crude and imperfect manner it is true, to reproduce his results.

From Telegraph to Telephone

Bell proceeded to educate himself about electricity—still a young field at the time. In studying the transmission of signals, Bell learned that telegraph engineers were trying to find a way to send several messages along a wire at the same time (see chapter 1, "Writing with Lightning.") By 1872, Bell had the beginnings of an idea for solving the problem.

Bell turned to his knowledge of how different sound pitches can be combined. He began to work on what he called a "harmonic telegraph." This device would allow several telegraph operators to send messages at the same time. Each message would have dots and dashes that sounded at a different pitch. Each receiver would respond only to the message to which it was tuned.

As Stephen Lubar recounts in *InfoCulture,* Bell soon realized that he might be able to do even more than use sound to separate telegraph messages:

> *If I can get a mechanism which will make a current of electricity vary in its intensity, as the air varies in density when a sound is passed through it, I can telegraph any sound, even the sound of speech.*

Bell had discovered the basic principle of the telephone. He now had to find financial backing to turn his idea into a commercial success. Bell had become friends with Gardiner Greene Hubbard, whose daughter Mabel had become one of his students in the school for the deaf. In 1875, Gardiner, Bell, and another friend, George Sanders, formed a partnership to develop and patent inventions.

Aided by a talented assistant, Thomas Watson, Bell began to experiment with the harmonic telegraph. Their device used steel reeds that could be vibrated by electromagnets. During June 1875, they worked to tune the reeds in the transmitter and receiver so that they could send messages.

One day, Watson tightened an adjustment screw a little too much, stopping the reed from moving. He plucked the reed to try to set it in motion again. Bell came running into the room and shouted that he had heard the sound of Watson's reed clearly.

The vibration of the reed had set up a corresponding vibration in the magnetic coil. This in turn had induced an electrical current in the wire without needing a battery at all. The current went to the electromagnet in the other instrument and vibrated it, which in turn vibrated the other reed, sounding a tone.

Importantly, this current was not the interrupted, on-and-off kind used in a telegraph but rather a continuous current that carried the pattern of the sound waves. As H. M. Boettinger quotes in *The Telephone Book,* Bell excitedly wrote to his parents that

> [a]t last a means had been found which will render possible the transmission . . . of the human voice . . . I am close to the land for which I am bound and when the fog lifts I shall see it right before me.

Gardiner Hubbard wanted Bell to finish the multiple telegraph first, so they could make money licensing it. But Bell found that he could not tear his mind away from the transmission of speech. Bell did have something else on his mind, though. He had gradually fallen in love with the 18-year-old Mabel and wanted to marry her. Hubbard at first refused to give his permission for the marriage unless Bell finished the multiple telegraph. Bell would not turn back. He and Mabel became engaged anyway, and work on the telephone continued furiously.

Bell replaced the reeds with a vibrating membrane, perhaps inspired by his knowledge of the human ear. By July, Bell was transmitting the sound of a human voice, though the actual words could not be made out. Bell had also learned about the work of rival inventor Elisha Gray, who also seemed close to making a working telephone. On February 14, 1876, Hubbard filed Bell's preliminary patent for a "speaking telephone." Only a few hours later, Gray arrived at the patent office to learn that Bell had beaten him to the punch.

Bell's patent was entitled merely "Improvements in Telegraphy." The real significance of the telephone was still unclear. Gray did not challenge Bell's patent at first, believing that the telephone was of no real commercial value. He soon regretted this belief.

Bell did get some clues as to how Gray's telephone worked, and he adopted Gray's idea of using a diaphragm that dipped a needle into a dish of slightly acid water as it vibrated in response to the sound of a voice. As the needle dipped in and out, the resistance of an electrical current changed, varying the current according to the sound pattern. On March 10, 1876, Watson went into another room to listen to the telephone receiver. As quoted by John Brooks in *Telephone: The First Hundred Years* (and many others), Watson recalled that

> *Almost at once, I was astonished to hear Bell's voice . . . distinctly saying "Mr. Watson, come here, I want you." . . . I rushed down the hall to his room and found that he had upset the acid of a battery over his clothes. He forgot his accident in his joy over the success of the new transmitter.*

The telephone was a reality.

The year 1876 was the centennial, or 100th birthday, of the United States. A great fair, the Centennial Exposition, was being held in Philadelphia. This fair included many technical marvels that celebrated American ingenuity. Bell used this national showcase to demonstrate his telephone to the public. According to legend, one astonished visitor, Brazilian emperor Don Pedro, exclaimed: "My God, it talks!"

Battling for Business

In considering his invention, Bell (as quoted by Steven Lubar) wrote:

> *The telephone reminds me of a child, only it grows much more rapidly. What is before it in the future, no man can tell—but I see new possibilities before it—and new uses.*

Bell saw the essential difference between the telegraph, which was a kind of super-speedy mail, and the telephone, which let people talk in "real time," with their own voice in a natural conversation. He believed that people would soon see the value of this kind of communication.

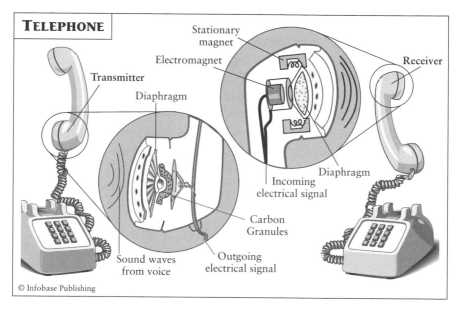

The telephone transmitter has a diaphragm that vibrates in response to the voice. This vibration compresses a carbon "button" to convert the sounds to a flow of electrical current. At the receiver, an electromagnet vibrates a diaphragm that in turn reproduces the original sound waves.

In 1877, Bell and his partners formed the Bell Telephone Association with a total investment of $500,000. They decided to lease telephones to customers rather than simply selling them. By keeping ownership of the equipment, Bell Telephone could set the standards for its use and make sure phone users could connect to one another.

One drawback of this plan was that the company would make less money right away than they would have gotten for selling the phones. The company struggled to get enough money to expand production. People who were willing to invest the money demanded and received more control of the company.

Gradually, Bell himself became less involved in the business. He went on to work on lesser-known but interesting inventions such as a surgical probe, a "photophone" that sent messages on a light beam, new kinds of kites, and sea-skimming hydroplane boats. Most of all,

Bell returned to his roots—his work on behalf of the deaf. Looking back on his life, according to historians Ellen Stern and Emily Gwathmey, Bell lamented to his friend Helen Keller that

> [i]t is a pity so many people make money the criterion of success. I wish my experiences had resulted in enabling the deaf to speak with less difficulty. That would have made me truly happy.

The real builder of the telephone's business empire was Theodore Vail, a younger relative of the Alfred Vail who had been so important in helping Morse develop his telegraph. Starting as a telegrapher for Western Union, Vail developed his skills as a business executive until he took charge of the Post Office Railway Mail Service. When Vail joined the Bell Company, in June 1878, it had 10,755 telephones in service.

OTHER INVENTORS: ELISHA GRAY

If things had worked out a little differently, Elisha Gray (1835–1901) might have been recognized as the inventor of the telephone. Gray made several inventions relating to the telegraph, including a device that could send and receive handwriting. Like Bell, Gray built a successful multiplex telegraph that used harmonic sound transmission, and he also discovered the basic principle of the telephone.

Unfortunately for Gray, he filed a patent notice for the telephone a few hours after Bell. Gray did not challenge Bell's patent until after the telephone had become successful. He then waged and lost a lengthy legal battle with Bell.

The story of Bell and Gray is a good example of the truth that few inventions truly have a single inventor. Usually, some innovative concept is "in the air," and several people may have grasped it. The "winner" of the invention race may be the person who had the most practical approach, persevered the longest, or was quickest to the patent office counter. Bell was perhaps all three.

The first problem Vail and the Bell Company faced was Vail's old employer, Western Union. The giant telegraph company had ignored the telephone at first, agreeing with Gray that it was unlikely to become an important product. But when the telephone started to become popular, Western Union bought rights to patents held by Gray and Thomas Edison (who had invented a carbon microphone that improved telephone transmission) and started its own telephone company. The Bell Company went to court, claiming that Western Union had infringed on Bell's patent. When courts began upholding Bell's patent because it was well documented and had been filed before Gray's, Western Union agreed to get out of the telephone business.

These great legal and financial battles signaled the beginning of a change in the role of the inventor in the later 19th century. Decisions made by the heads of giant corporations had become as important to the development of an invention as the solutions to technical problems.

I WAS THERE: HELEN KELLER AND ALEXANDER GRAHAM BELL: BREAKING THE SILENCE

When she was only 19 months old, Helen Keller (1880–1968) was robbed of both sight and hearing by a brain infection. Teaching her to communicate seemed to be impossible. Still, Helen's doctor urged her father to take her to Alexander Graham Bell, who had a reputation as a superb teacher of the deaf.

According to author Judith St. George, Keller later recalled her first meeting with Bell. "He held me on his knee while I examined his watch, and he made it strike for me. He understood my signs, and I knew it and loved him at once." They would become lifelong friends and overcome many obstacles in her future education.

When Keller wrote her autobiography, she dedicated it "To Alexander Graham Bell, who taught the deaf to speak and enabled the listening ear to hear speech from the Atlantic to the Rockies."

Long Distance

In its early years, the telephone faced two obstacles to its more widespread use. One was the need to improve the equipment so that voices could be heard clearly regardless of the distance. The first public advertisement for phone service noted:

> [O]n first listening on the telephone although the sound is perfectly audible, the articulation seems to be indistinct, but after a few trials, the ear becomes accustomed to the peculiar sound and finds little difficulty in understanding the words.

Like most advertising, this overstated things. Early telephone users often had to shout or ask the other person to repeat something.

Bell's first commercial telephone turned the voice into a small electrical current that quickly became weak with distance. Edison, however, came up with the idea of using a vibrating button of carbon to vary an existing current from a battery, thus making a stronger phone signal. Edison also invented a telephone receiver that could amplify the incoming signal.

As with the telegraph, long-distance telephone lines needed some way to keep the signal from fading out as the line "soaked up" the electricity through a process called capacitance. In 1894, Professor Michael Pupin of Columbia University invented the "loading coil." This device used induction (the creation of current in a magnetic field) to counteract the loss of current through capacitance. Finally, as with the telegraph, a way was found to amplify a signal and "repeat" it from one part of the line to the next. The most effective amplifier or repeater used a new invention, Lee De Forest's vacuum tube (see chapter 5, "Triumph and Tragedy").

In 1915, Bell repeated his famous first telephone message "Mr. Watson, come here, I want you!" But Bell was in New York, and Watson was in San Francisco. Watson replied to Bell that this time it would take him a week to fulfill his request!

Getting Connected

Building the lines and strengthening the phone signals was only half the battle. The other side of the problem of establishing a universal phone service was setting up connections so people could talk to one another. The first phone switchboards used improvised equipment to connect subscribers. Authors Stern and Gwathmey recount that at the very first exchange in New Haven, Connecticut:

> [W]ire from discarded bustles [frames used under women's garments] was used, and in another switchboard placed in service in Meriden, a short time later, teapot cover handles and carriage bolts were successfully used to complete essential parts.

Telephone exchanges soon adopted the "crossbar" switchboard consisting of vertical and horizontal bars to which all the subscribers' lines were connected. To make a call, a phone user picked up the phone and told the operator the name (or later, number) of the desired party. The switchboard operator plugged one end of a cord from a socket for the caller's line, and the other into the socket for the other telephone.

This worked tolerably well when the phone exchange had no more than 50 or so subscribers. To handle more users, the "multiple switchboard" was invented in 1883. This allowed any operator at any switchboard to make a connection that would go through to subscribers on other switchboards. Nevertheless, the need to make all connections by hand made service slower and less reliable as traffic increased.

Harold Sharlin quotes an observer who reported that in an early telephone exchange:

> The racket was almost deafening. Boys are rushing madly hither and thither, while others are putting in or taking out pegs from a central framework as if they were lunatics engaged in a game of fox and geese.

By 1881, the phone companies started replacing male switchboard operators with women. According to one supervisor, "[their] service is much superior to that of boys and men. They are steadier, do not drink beer, and are always on hand."

What this official did not say was that women could also be paid about half the wages that men received.

In 1892, Almon B. Strowger, a Kansas City undertaker, invented the automatic switching system. Instead of using crossbars, the phone lines were connected to rotary switches that were linked by electromagnetic relays. The person making the call selected the number by turning the dial on the telephone. The dial sent pulses to the relays that automatically turned the switches to make the connection.

Changing Social Customs

When the telephone first appeared, many people thought the device would be used mainly in pairs (such as between offices and warehouses) and left connected all day. This brought up the problem of how to notifiy a person when it was time for a conversation. Bell himself answered the telephone by shouting "Ahoy!" like a sailor calling to another ship. Thomas Edison, however, favored "Hello," which became the most common phone greeting, even after bells were provided to signal incoming calls.

As telephones came into more common use in domestic as well as business settings, a problem of etiquette also arose. In 19th-century American society (at least in the upper classes), people did not just meet—they had to be introduced. With the telephone, however, strangers could introduce themselves and carry on business without meeting at a particular place. This took some getting used to, but the advantages for business were clear. Managers in a main office could directly supervise employees in a district office. This development contributed to the centralization of business in the national corporations that increasingly dominated the economy.

The telephone completed the speedup of the pace of business begun by the telegraph. Unlike the telegraph, however, the telephone also sped up social interaction. A picnic or dinner party could be organized without having to send and receive letters. Teenagers could make dates or just talk without having a chaperone.

Perhaps the most important effect of the telephone, however, was the way it expanded the role of women. Three million women worked for the Bell System in its first 100 years. In the business world, male secretaries were largely replaced by women whose telephone (and typewriting) skills made them the lifeline of business. As more women became able to earn their own living, they were better able to assert their independence.

The telephone also helped reduce the social isolation of women who remained at home. This was particularly true in rural areas, where many farms might share a single "party line" that was an effective way to keep up with the gossip of the community.

The Telephone in the Digital Age

The telephone industry was the first to make systematic, ongoing research part of its business plans. In 1925, several different research laboratories were brought together into Bell Telephone Laboratories.

In the 1940s, the vast movement of people and resources during World War II strained the capacity of the phone system (see chapter 7, "Unlocking the Signals"). By the 1950s, there were 50 million phones in the United States alone.

The war had also brought about an electronics revolution that would help the phone system meet the challenges. During the 1950s, the newly invented transistor began to replace vacuum tubes in amplifiers and switches. Transistors were faster, more reliable, more compact, and used less power. In the 1960s, radio technology (through microwave links and communications satellites) had reduced the system's dependence on copper wire.

The need to be able to connect all the parts of a rapidly growing system led to the harnessing of computer technology. Computer-controlled switches could route connections quickly, bypassing blockages.

But having this vast system controlled by a single corporate structure made people increasingly uneasy. It had brought fulfillment of Theodore Vail's original goal of "One system with a common policy, common purpose, and common action." The phone company had escaped the breakup of the big business trusts in steel, oil, and railroads in the early part of the 20th century. In 1913, a compromise was reached in which the telephone monopoly would be allowed to continue in exchange for having its prices set by local regulation.

But in the rapidly changing, increasingly flexible electronic world of the 1960s and 1970s, the phone company seemed increasingly opposed to change. (In 1970, comedian Lily Tomlin's huffy "phone lady" on *Rowan and Martin's Laugh-In* became famous for her line, "We're the phone company. We don't care; we don't have to.")

Bell, through its Western Electric subsidiary, controlled the production of phone equipment. Devices from other manufacturers could not be connected without "Ma Bell's" approval. Many people began to feel that if the telephone giant were broken up into smaller companies and outsiders allowed to compete, consumers would have more choices of phone service at lower cost. In 1982, a federal judge agreed, and in 1984, the breakup of the Bell System began.

By then, the vast phone system was being called upon to fulfill another task: the transmission of data to and from online bulletin boards, information services, and the growing Internet. In a way, it was remarkable that a system that was not designed for such transmission worked as well as it did. Although the limited bandwidth of standard phone service soon frustrated computer users, clever engineers were able to come up with a new form of phone connection called DSL (digital subscriber line) that could carry data far more rapidly.

Today there is a bewildering choice of phone equipment and service plans. The telephone and computer have become even more tightly woven together through the Internet. Unlike the vanishing telegraph, the phone has mutated into new forms, such as wireless text messaging (see chapter 10, "Living in Cyberspace.") At the same time, voice phone calls can now be carried over the Internet where they may never meet a conventional wired phone line. And if they were alive now, Bell would simply have Watson carry a cell phone so he could be summoned anywhere.

Chronology

1847	Alexander Graham Bell is born in Edinburgh, Scotland
1863	Bell and his brother build an artificial voice box

1871–73	Bell studies sound and teaches at schools for the deaf
1872	Bell begins work on the "harmonic telegraph"
1875	Having accidentally discovered sound transmission, Bell turns from telegraph development to the telephone
1876	Bell patents and demonstrates the telephone
1877	The Bell Telephone Company is founded
1878	Theodore Vail joins the Bell company; he will soon lead it in the battle to control the nation's phone system
	Thomas Edison invents an improved telephone transmitter using a carbon microphone
1892	Almon B. Strowger invents the first automatic switchboard and dial phone
1915	Transcontinental phone service begins
1963	Touch-tone (push button) phones are introduced
1976	The first fully computerized phone switching systems are introduced
1982	A federal court orders the breakup of the Bell System
1990s	Regular and DSL (digital subscriber line) phone connections carry huge volumes of data on the Internet
	Cordless and cell phones change the way people use the telephone
2000s	Text messaging via cell phone and "voice over Internet" service become popular

Further Reading

Books

Boettinger, H. M. *The Telephone Book: Bell, Watson, Vail and American Life, 1876–1976.* Croton-on-Hudson, N.Y.: Riverwood Publishers, 1977.

> An illustrated history that puts the telephone in the context of the role technology has played in American society.

Brooks, John. *Telephone: The First Hundred Years.* New York: Harper & Row, 1975.
> Deals mainly with the development of the telephone industry.

Lubar, Stephen. *InfoCulture: The Smithsonian Book of Information Age Inventions.* Boston: Houghton Mifflin, 1993.
> Includes an account of Bell's invention of the telephone.

St. George, Judith. *Dear Dr. Bell . . . Your Friend, Helen Keller.* New York: William Morrow, 1993.
> The inspiring story of how Alexander Graham Bell helped Helen Keller, leading to a lifelong friendship.

Sharlin, Harold I. *The Making of the Electrical Age.* New York: Abelard-Schuman, 1964.
> An account of electrical inventors and inventions.

Stern, Ellen, and Emily Gwathmey. *Once upon a Telephone: An Illustrated Social History.* New York: Harcourt, Brace & Company, 1994.
> A wonderfully illustrated and narrated account of how the telephone influenced American life.

Web Sites

"Alexander Graham Bell's Path to the Telephone." Available online. URL: http://www3.iath.virginia.edu/albell/homepage.html. Accessed on December 10, 2005.
> A detailed, interactive journey through Bell's process of invention.

"Bell System Memorial." Available online. URL: http://www.bell systemmemorial.com. Accessed on February 8, 2006.
> Contains accounts and materials relating to the people, history, and technology of the Bell telephone system prior to its 1984 breakup.

Bellis, Mary. "The History of the Telephone." About.com. Available online. URL: http://inventors.about.com/library/inventors/bltele phone.htm. Accessed on February 8, 2006.
> Narrative history of the telephone, with many links to biographies of Bell, descriptions of telephone technology, and original documents.

THE MEDIA OF MEMORY

THOMAS EDISON, SOUND RECORDING, AND MOTION PICTURES

The telegraph and the telephone make instant communication possible. People do not communicate only in the here and now, though. They also set down thoughts, feelings, and images that become part of an ongoing conversation that can pass from generation to generation. The printed book has carried on such a dialogue for more than 500 years. About 150 years ago, photography added the ability to freeze an image in time for future eyes to see.

Sound and movement could not be recorded until just over a 100 years ago. The work of Thomas Edison and later inventors brought about the development of the phonograph and of motion pictures. These inventions made the past available in a new way. Today people can play a cylinder and hear words spoken by a president or sung by an opera singer a century ago. They can look at a screen and watch a flickering screen of people rushing along crowded streets, living in a world that vanished before their parents were born.

Young Entrepreneur

Thomas Alva Edison is the Tiger Woods of inventors—at his best, he is in a league of his own. In more than 50 years of work, he filed more than a 1,000 patents, setting a record that no individual is likely to beat in today's team-oriented corporate world.

Edison was born in Milan, Ohio, on February 11, 1847, though his family later moved to Port Huron, Michigan. Only a few months after beginning school at the age of 8, Edison found himself being constantly scolded by the teacher for not paying attention in class. He ran away from school and was taught at home by his mother. He also began to lose much of his hearing, perhaps because of an infection.

There was nothing wrong with Edison's sight, though, and he became an avid reader, soaking up knowledge on any subject that interested him. Indeed, Edison's hearing disability may have actually helped him develop his legendary concentration and work habits by shutting out distractions.

At the age of 12, Edison left home and became a "news butcher" on the railroad. News butchers sold food, candy, and newspapers to train passengers. With his earnings, he put together a small chemistry lab in which he performed experiments that sometimes got him in trouble with railroad conductors. (One unconfirmed story says Edison's hearing was further damaged when his ears were boxed by an angry conductor after one of his chemical experiments started a fire in a train car.) Like today's technically minded teenagers, Edison found himself to be at home in a rapidly changing, always moving world.

Thomas Edison was the superstar of American inventors. Among other achievements, he is credited with the electric light, the phonograph, and motion pictures. (U.S. Department of the Interior, National Park Service, Edison National Historic Site)

First Inventions

When he was 16, Edison encountered the invention that, together with the railroad, defined "high tech" in 19th-century America. He learned to be a telegrapher and soon began to tinker with telegraph equipment. Edison also tapped into the news being transmitted to railway stations and developed his own little newspaper—typeset, printed, and sold entirely aboard the train—which gained about 300 subscribers.

Edison's first major invention, at age 21, was an automatic stock ticker that used telegraph signals to send prices from the floor of the New York Stock Exchange to brokers' offices. When he received $40,000 for his invention, Edison established a laboratory at Newark, New Jersey (later moved to Menlo Park, New Jersey). From then on, Edison would be a full-time inventor.

One reason why Edison was so successful as an inventor was that he had the kind of mind that let him pursue several investigations at the same time, borrowing ideas from one to help with another. For example, during the early 1870s, Edison began studying how to improve the transatlantic telegraph. To aid in this work, he tried to build a tabletop model that would have the same electrical characteristics as the actual cable. When he tried to use carbon connectors to get the correct amount of electrical resistance, however, he found that the slightest vibration of the table or even a nearby sound would make the resistance change. He temporarily gave up the project.

Later in the decade, however, Edison began working on an improved microphone. He tried many materials for the microphone without success. He then remembered how sensitive to vibrations the carbon contacts in his table model had been. Edison built a microphone that used carbon buttons to convert the vibrations from the sound-catching diaphragm to change the electrical current. The result was a big improvement in Bell's telephone. Edison's earlier failure had become the basis for later success.

Edison's ability to visualize and adapt new ideas was matched by his stamina. Like today's Silicon Valley software developers, Edison regularly worked for days on end with only occasional naps. He would later say that turning ideas into inventions was "1 percent inspiration and 99 percent perspiration."

Frozen Sound

Although Edison is most remembered for his invention of the electric light and power system, when asked which of his inventions was his favorite, he always answered, "the phonograph." Its almost magical ability to record and re-create something as fleeting as sound seemed to fascinate both Edison and the popular imagination.

In the fall of 1877, Edison was, as usual, working on several different projects. He was trying to make a loudspeaker that would make it easier to hear telephone calls. Edison also had a contract with Western Union, who wanted devices that could automatically record or copy telegrams and perhaps voices from the telephone.

One day, according to his chief assistant Charles Batchelor as quoted in V. K. Chew's book *Talking Machines*:

> *Mr. Edison had a telephone diaphragm mounted in a mouthpiece of rubber in his hand, and he was sounding notes in front of it and feeling the vibration at the center of the diaphragm with his finger. After amusing himself with this for some time, he turned around to me and he said: "Batch, if we had a point on this, we could make a record on some material which we could afterwards pull under the point and it would give us the speech back."*

They immediately tried the experiment by attaching a stylus, or needle, to the diaphragm and passing a strip of waxed paper under it while shouting into the device. "Batchelor and I listened breathlessly," Edison later recalled. "We heard a distinct sound, which a strong imagination might have translated as the original Halloo!" Although it was not yet in practical form, the phonograph had been born.

Interestingly, this invention had been a "near miss" for an earlier inventor named Leon Scott. In 1857, Scott had built a device he called the phonautograph. It used a diaphragm and a stylus to trace a record of sound vibrations on a piece of smoked glass—but there was no way to play them back. Edison and Bell both knew about this invention, but they drew different conclusions about it. Bell noticed how the diaphragm could transmit distinctive sound vibrations, and that helped lead him to develop the telephone. Edison, however, focused on the record tracings and thought about how they could be turned back into the original sound.

Bell was chagrined when he heard that Edison had invented a phonograph. Author Steven Lubar quotes Bell as exclaiming that "It is a most astonishing thing to me that I could possibly have let this invention slip through my fingers when I consider how my thoughts have been directed to this subject for so many years past." Indeed, the main difference between the telephone and the phonograph is in whether the sound vibrations are transmitted or recorded.

Creating the Phonograph

Having announced his invention, Edison then went to work making a practical instrument. For some time, he had been working on an "embossing telegraph" that recorded telegraph messages on a revolving paper-covered cylinder, using the mechanism of one of his earlier inventions, the "electromotograph." Something clicked in Edison's mind. Why not record the sound of the human voice on the cylinder?

Edison attached a funnel to a diaphragm to help pick up the sound. He found that substituting tinfoil for paper on the surface of the cylinder made the sound more distinct. To test his new machine, he shouted a nursery rhyme into the funnel—"Mary had a little lamb, its fleece was white as snow. And everywhere that Mary went, the lamb was sure to go"—while turning the crank.

The tinfoil was now covered with a series of "bumps" corresponding to the sounds from his voice. To play back the message, he pulled back the funnel and stylus attachment and swung a second playback stylus so it just touched the cylinder. As he cranked the machine again, the stylus passed over the foil and reproduced the original sounds.

As quoted by Neil Baldwin in *Edison: Inventing the Century,* Edison recalled that he "was never so taken aback in all my life. . . . I was always afraid of anything that worked the first time." He was now ready to patent the phonograph.

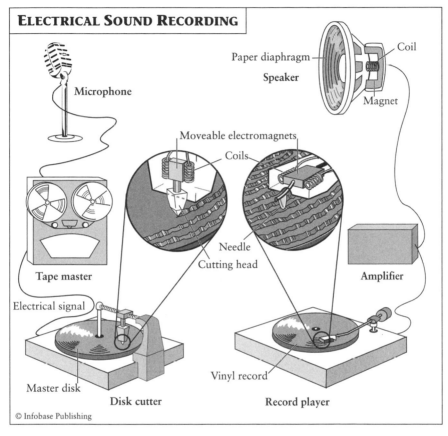

ELECTRICAL SOUND RECORDING

Coil

Paper diaphragm

Speaker

Magnet

Microphone

Moveable electromagnets

Coils

Needle

Cutting head

Tape master

Amplifier

Electrical signal

Master disk

Disk cutter

Vinyl record

Record player

© Infobase Publishing

To record sound, an electrical signal from a microphone or a master recording tape causes varying magnetism in the electromagnets on the cutting head. The recording stylus cuts a wavy track in a master record, which is then reproduced. To play the record, the phonograph stylus follows the grooves, creating a varying current that is amplified to drive a speaker.

The Battle for the Living Room

Edison's first public demonstration of the phonograph was held in the offices of *Scientific American* magazine. One of its columnists wrote with amazement that "the machine inquired as to our health, asked us how we like the phonograph, informed us that *it* was very well, and bid us a cordial good night."

Following his usual habit, Edison did some brainstorming and, according to Robert Conot in *A Streak of Luck,* Edison poured forth into his notebook a torrent of ideas about possible uses for his invention even before he had perfected it:

> *I propose to apply the phonograph to make Dolls speak sing cry & make various sounds also apply it to all kinds of Toys . . . to reproduce from sheets music both orchestral and instrument & vocal . . . A family may have one machine & 1000 sheets of the music thus giving endless amusement. I also propose to make toy music boxes & toy talking boxes playing several tunes also to clocks and watches for calling out the time of day or waking a person for advertisements rotated continuously by clockwork. . . .*

Edison and his partners formed the Edison Speaking Phonograph Company to market the invention, but Edison's attention for the next four years would be taken up by the electric light and the establishment of power-generating systems. Meanwhile, Alexander Graham Bell began to come up with different kinds of phonograph mechanisms that would not be covered by Edison's patent. One of these used a jet of air instead of a needle to make impressions on the record. Bell filed competing patents for what he called the "graphophone."

By 1888, the electric light system had been finished, and Edison responded to Bell's challenge by putting his "invention factory" into high gear. Edison's team of 100 researchers looked for ways to improve every part of the machine. They found a coating for the cylinder that worked better than the fragile tinfoil, and they added a spring-powered motor so it would not have to be cranked by hand.

At first, Edison marketed the phonograph as a business machine for recording phone messages or dictation. The first model was described by one listener as sounding "like a partially educated parrot with a sore throat and a cold in the head." Though the machines gradually improved, it was many years before most businesses accepted them.

Finally, though, Edison turned to what is today the most obvious use of the phonograph—musical entertainment. Edison and his assistants put a phonograph in a box with a coin slot to attract passersby in hotel lobbies or special arcades. By 1891, about 1,000 of these one-record jukeboxes were in operation. It was a modest moneymaker and a great way to introduce the phonograph to millions of people who had never heard it before.

The next step was to market phonographs for the home, and it looked like people were ready for this new form of entertainment. By the turn of the 20th century, there were about 800,000 phonographs in homes in the United States, and the production of records was soaring. The first "gold record" in the industry was a recording of the opera *I Pagliacci* by superstar singer Enrico Caruso that sold over 1 million copies.

A new competitor, a German-American inventor named Emil Berliner, entered the scene. Berliner invented a phonograph that used a disk record rather than Edison's cylinder. Edison had rejected disks earlier because the cylinder had better sound quality and the needle moved over the cylinder at a constant speed, avoiding distortion in the playback.

The disk, however, had one huge advantage. With cylinders, the record producer had to line up several recording phonographs in front of the singer or band. The performers had to keep repeating the piece of music in front of the assembled phonographs to produce a small batch of records.

The disk, on the other hand, could be copied by etching the original recording with acid, stamping its pattern on a master disk, and using the master to press out many records. Berliner's phonograph was also louder than Edison's, which made it better for filling a whole room with music, even if the sound quality was not as good.

As shown in so many of his inventions, Edison had the ability to focus on one problem and keep working on it until it was solved. But the flip side of this strength of personality was a kind of rigidity that meant he stubbornly kept trying to improve a technology that had already become obsolete. In response to Berliner's disks, Edison came out with an improved cylinder that had better sound quality and that could play for four minutes instead of two. Unfortunately, the new cylinders would not work in the old machines and did not sell well.

Finally, Edison bowed to the inevitable and developed his own disk phonograph. His thoroughness again showed itself as he poured several million dollars into designing an all-new system.

The Phonograph Goes Electric

During the "jazz age" of the 1920s, the phonograph encountered a major competitor—the radio (see chapter 5, "Triumph and Tragedy"). Once someone bought a radio, unlimited music could be had for the cost of a few pennies worth of electricity. During the depression decade of the 1930s, this was a real bargain.

The radio also helped the phonograph, however. Radio stations began to play records on the air, encouraging record sales. Also, the electronic technology behind the radio could be adapted to the phonograph. Improved microphones and electronic tube amplifiers gave the new electric record players a fuller and richer sound.

During the 1920s, the phonograph helped African Americans preserve and enjoy their blues and jazz heritage. (Library of Congress)

SOCIAL IMPACT: PRESERVING MUSICAL HERITAGE

The phonograph and sound recording, along with radio, created a mass entertainment industry. The big record companies (and nearly all radio stations) were not interested in recording ethnic music such as the blues of rural African Americans, the lively klezmer tunes of Yiddish America, or the folk ballads of Appalachia. But as recording equipment became cheaper and more portable, small companies were able to produce blues, jazz, and other records that kept traditional music alive and inspired a new generation of musicians to build upon it.

Aided by government grants during the 1930s, researchers went to rural areas to collect examples of blues, country music, and folk ballads. Without these efforts, this generation's knowledge of the evolution of American popular music would be much less complete.

Electrical recording had a more subtle effect on how people listened to music. As author Steven Lubar points out:

> Reactions to [recorded music] were also based on changing standards of taste in music, and on changing ideas about what music reproduction should be. These changes had come about because of the radio, because of new kinds of music, because the phonograph had changed music, and perhaps most important, because the increasing predominance of recording had changed the place of music in peoples' lives.

While record sales did not regain real momentum until the war years of the early 1940s, in 1947 400 million records would be sold to American consumers.

New Technologies for Sound Recording

The 1940s and 1950s brought a number of improvements in sound recording. The LP, or "long-playing," record, introduced in 1948, could hold up to 23 minutes on each side of the record. Lovers of classical music could now listen to long symphonic movements without interruption. The small 45 rpm record was also introduced about this time. It became popular in the 1950s because it held one popular song three minutes or so in length. This was a perfect fit for the radio stations that played the exciting new rock-and-roll music at a frenetic pace set by a disk jockey.

There were also continuing improvements in sound quality. Inventors had been working on stereo recording for years. Early

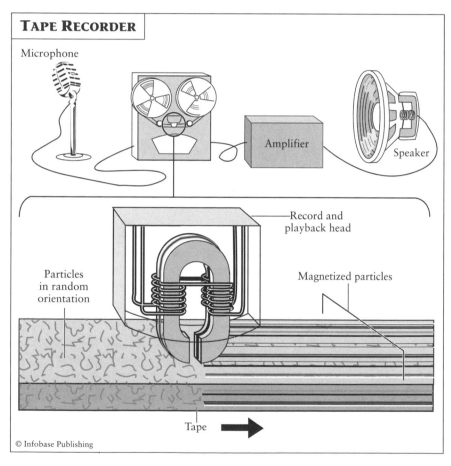

TAPE RECORDER

Microphone

Amplifier

Speaker

Record and playback head

Particles in random orientation

Magnetized particles

Tape

© Infobase Publishing

In tape recording, the electrical signal from the sound source is used by the electromagnet in the recording head to magnetize a pattern of metal particles in the tape. For playback, the magnetism sensed from the tape is turned back into an electrical signal that is amplified and used to drive a speaker.

systems needed to record both the left and right sound tracks separately, which meant that the record could hold only half as much music. But inventors learned to combine an up-and-down track with a side-to-side one so that both left and right sound channels were recorded in the same record groove.

During World War II, the Germans perfected tape recording, where the signal from a microphone is fed to an electromagnetic recording head that magnetizes metal particles in a tape in a pattern that corresponds to the sound. Tape recording led, in the 1960s, to affordable portable recorders, tape players for cars, and, in the 1980s, to the Walkman and similar lightweight units that let people "wear" their music.

Tape recording had an important effect on the recording industry. It made it possible for recording engineers to record sound from four, eight, 16 or more separate microphones, each on its own track on the tape. Using mixing technology, the recording engineer adjusted the sound characteristics of the performance and added special effects. The Beatles' landmark 1967 recording *Sgt. Pepper's Lonely Hearts Club Band* showed how a recording could be a complete package of sound in which it was no longer possible to separate the work of the musician from that of the engineer.

In the 1980s, recorded music entered the computer age as compact disks (CDs) replaced the vinyl phonograph record. Compact disk recording turns sound into thousands of numbers a second, each representing the size (amplitude) of the sound wave at an instant in time. The data is "burned" into the compact disk in coded patterns by a laser, which is also used to retrieve the information and feed it to the playback mechanism. Compact disks have none of the surface noise of vinyl records, and they do not wear out with repeated play. Some critics, however, believe that reducing sound to numbers may remove some of its more subtle qualities.

The digitization of sound continued at the turn of the 21st century with the storing of digitized sound files (such as MP3s) on portable devices such as the popular Apple iPod. Thousands of songs can now be stored in a space the size of a matchbox.

Digitization has made all sound available for modification, regardless of its original source. Modern musicians (particularly in hip-hop) are free to "sample" any sound source and use it as

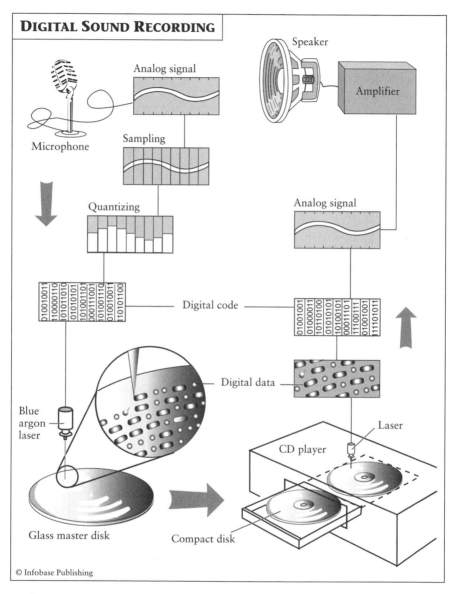

DIGITAL SOUND RECORDING

Speaker

Analog signal

Amplifier

Microphone

Sampling

Quantizing

Analog signal

Digital code

Digital data

Blue argon laser

Laser

CD player

Glass master disk

Compact disk

© Infobase Publishing

Today most sound recording is digital, as with compact disks (CDs). A laser creates a pattern of dots and spaces corresponding to numeric sound levels. This is then reproduced on compact disks in the form of pits and flat areas. For playback, the pattern of reflected laser light is turned back into numeric data that is then converted to a sound signal.

raw material for new musical compositions. However, the freeing of music from a fixed recorded abode has also set off fierce battles between recording companies and users who wish to freely copy and distribute music using file-sharing services. (It is likely that Edison would not have approved of Napster.)

Moving Pictures

The same explosion of ideas and invention that make the late 19th century so exciting in the history of technology can be seen in the birth of the movies. The idea behind motion pictures is something called "persistence of vision." This means that the human brain continues to "see" an image for about a tenth of a second after it is no longer in front of the eye. The illusion of movement is created by showing drawings or photographs in rapid succession. Because the time gap between pictures is much shorter than the brain's persistence

---

OTHER INVENTORS: THE LUMIÈRE BROTHERS

Louis-Jean Lumière (1864–1948) and Auguste-Marie-Louis-Nicolas Lumière (1862–1954) invented the Cinematographe, a combination movie camera, developer, and film projector. (One of their key ideas was to use toothed wheels [sprockets] to engage holes in the edge of the film to pull it through the machine.) The word *cinema* for motion pictures comes from the Greek word *kinema,* meaning motion. Movie theaters in Europe are often called cinemas.

The Lumières began showing programs of two-minute films in theaters in 1895. Their films often recorded scenes from daily life, such as workers leaving a factory. They also invented the newsreel—a film devoted to current events that was popular until television became widespread in the 1950s.

Ironically, by the turn of the 20th century, the Lumières had decided that there was no future in motion pictures, and they turned their attention to developing color photography and new film products.

At the turn of the 20th century, people could play a record or see a short film by dropping a coin into a machine. (Smithsonian Institution Photo No. 87-1615)

time, the empty space between pictures is never seen. The viewer sees what appears to be a single, moving image.

Once there is a succession of images, they have to be projected in rapid succession to create a moving picture. Eadweard Muybridge invented a device he called the Zoopraxiscope. It was a disk that had a series of drawings around the edge. When it turned, it produced an animated image, such as a horse running or a clown dancing. The French inventor Etienne-Jules Marey adopted the Zoopraxiscope idea by projecting through the turning disk to create a moving image from still photos.

In 1888, Edison and Muybridge met to discuss how they might combine the Zoopraxiscope with a phonograph to create moving pictures with sound. Edison assigned his assistant William Dickson to the project. The result of their work was a device called the Kinetoscope. They replaced the whirling disk, which could hold only a few dozen pictures, with a strip of film that had holes punched along the edges, so it could be pulled through the projector to show the moving pictures. (For the time being, they dropped the idea of having sound.)

As with the phonograph, Edison first marketed the Kinetoscope as a coin-operated device. The viewer inserted a nickel, looked through the viewing hole, and saw about 15 seconds of film.

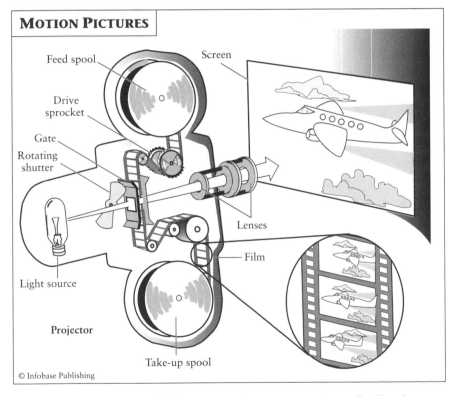

MOTION PICTURES

Feed spool
Screen
Drive sprocket
Gate
Rotating shutter
Light source
Lenses
Film
Projector
Take-up spool

© Infobase Publishing

Both the movie camera and film projector have a motor that pulls film along from reel to reel using gears that engage holes along the edges of the film. In the camera, the moving film is exposed as it passes through the lens and the shutter clicks. In the projector, the developed frames of the film are passed between a bright light and a lens and appear on the screen so quickly that the eye does not distinguish the individual images.

The novelty of the Kinetoscope soon wore off. Edison, along with the Lumière brothers in France, began in 1895 to build projectors that could show short films to a theater audience instead of a single viewer. The theaters charged only a nickel for admission, so they were called nickelodeons. By 1909, the movie industry was thriving. In the United States, more than 100 companies were producing more than 2,000 films a year.

It is hard for 21st-century readers to realize what a powerful impact motion pictures had on society at the start of the last century. Even the crude movies of the time looked so real that people in the audience sometimes ran in terror when they saw a train coming at them on the screen. But as people learned to appreciate the new entertainment medium, going to the movies became a popular social activity for people of all ages. The rise of Hollywood and the creation of glamorous movie stars became important parts of popular culture.

Edison had played a pioneering role in working out the mechanics of movie production, including building the Black Maria, a shed that served as one of the first movie studios. But as with the phonograph and music, Edison became less relevant as artistry began to become at least as important as technology.

Movies Grow Up

In 1915, the American director D.W. Griffith produced *The Birth of a Nation,* a three-hour feature movie that developed a complex narrative and pioneered modern techniques such as close-ups and a truck-mounted "tracking" camera that followed the action. (The film's contents were controversial and troubling: The movie glorified the post–Civil War Ku Klux Klan and helped inspire a revival of the racist organization.)

Other movie directors such as Cecil B. DeMille and the Russian Sergei Eisenstein began to see themselves as creative artists working in a medium that could be as significant as literature or music.

The 1920s brought a practical way to add sound to the movies. Before then, movies were often accompanied by an organist, but all words spoken by characters had to be indicated by a panel of text on the screen. The first major "talking" movie, *The Jazz Singer* of 1927, used a special phonograph that had to be started by an operator when cued by a particular scene in the film. This awkward approach was soon replaced by a system that used a pattern of gray spots along the side of the film. Instead of being projected on the screen, this pattern was passed through a photoelectric cell that converted it into a sound signal.

The effort to add color to the movies took longer and was more difficult. At first, important frames in a film were often hand-tinted by artists. In 1935, a system called Technicolor began to be popular; perhaps the best-known early color film was *The Wizard of Oz* in 1939. But difficulty in getting the color to look natural, as well as expense, kept the majority of movies in black and white until the 1950s.

During the 1950s, sales in movie theaters were threatened by a new way to show moving pictures: television (see chapter 5, "The Ghost Light"). Moviemakers responded to this threat by making movies more like theater plays, by dealing with themes too complex or "adult" for TV and by creating panoramic epics that could only be appreciated on the big screen.

In 1977, director George Lucas's epic *Star Wars* series began, combining fantasy, high-tech computer-generated imagery, and powerful visual and sound effects. Today visual images are often stored as data that can be manipulated by computer-based tools to create animation far more realistic than can be achieved by filming physical models set to a series of poses.

Meanwhile, the camcorder (film-based or digital), "webcams," and even video cell phones have given ordinary people unprecedented ability to record and transmit events as dramatic as the onrushing wave of the 2005 Asian tsunami. Amateur filmmakers can now buy relatively inexpensive tools that are far more capable than those that major studios had back in the 1980s.

Edison's Legacy

The sound and visual media Edison pioneered have greatly changed in over a century, but the fundamental ideas that he either discovered (or more often, adapted or improved) still remain recognizable. Any one of Edison's major inventions could have been the capstone for the career of any other inventor, but perhaps Edison's most enduring legacy was not an invention but a new *process* of invention. Edison's Menlo Park, New Jersey, laboratory was the first facility designed to continually search for, develop, and refine new ideas, turning them into marketable products. This model was soon adopted by industrial laboratories in the United States and Europe, such as the Bell Telephone Laboratories.

The nearly deaf and often impatient and irascible Edison could be very difficult to work for, and Edison's family life suffered from the lack of attention he gave his wife, Mina, and their children. Only in his last years did Edison seem to become comfortable with domestic life.

By the 1920s, Edison was an authentic American hero, held forth as a model of the nation's ingenuity and resourcefulness, along with Henry Ford. The "Wizard of Menlo Park" died on October 18, 1931. In his honor, electric lights were briefly turned off in many cities around the world.

Chronology

1847	Thomas Edison is born in Milan, Ohio, on February 11
1870	Edison makes his first major invention, an automatic stock ticker
1877	Edison builds a working phonograph using a tinfoil-covered cylinder
1893	Edison introduces the coin-operated Kinetoscope to show brief films
1895	Edison and the Lumière brothers begin showing films in theaters
1901	Edison's studio produces *The Great Train Robbery*, the first film to have a lengthy narrative
1915	D.W. Griffith's *Birth of a Nation* helps demonstrate modern movie-camera techniques
1920s	Sound tracks are added to movies; phonographs use electric motors and tube amplifiers for fuller sound

1930s	The Great Depression hurts phonograph sales, as people turn to radio for entertainment
1931	Thomas Edison dies on October 18
1948	The long-playing (LP) record allows recording of longer works
1949	The 45 rpm record is introduced; it becomes the preferred format for popular music
1950s	"Hi-fi" becomes a popular hobby, and stereo begins to be introduced; movie producers respond to the challenge of television by introducing more sophisticated movies, epics, and greater use of color
1967	The Beatles' album *Sgt. Pepper's Lonely Hearts Club Band* demonstrates new sound-mixing and production techniques
1977	*Star Wars* signals a new era in movie special-effects epics
1980s	Compact disks (CDs) replace vinyl records; camcorders allow for easy creation of amateur videos
Late 1990s	Sharing of music and video files on the Internet threatens recording-industry profits and leads to legal battles
2000s	Solid-state digital music players (such as MP3 players and the Apple iPod) become popular

Further Reading

Books

Baldwin, Neil. Edison: Inventing the Century. New York: Hyperion, 1995.
> A lively and poignant biography of Thomas Edison, America's most prolific inventor, suggesting ways in which his inventions virtually defined "modernity."

Conot, Robert. *A Streak of Luck*. New York: Seaview Books, 1979.
> A biography that challenges the legends of Edison's life with newly uncovered material.

Gleasner, Diana C. *The Movies*. New York: Walker, 1983.
> A history of film for young people.

Lubar, Stephen. *InfoCulture: The Smithsonian Book of Information Age Inventions.* Boston: Houghton Mifflin, 1993.
> Includes some coverage of Edison (particularly the phonograph and motion pictures.)

Pretzer, William S., ed. *Working at Inventing: Thomas A. Edison and the Menlo Park Experience.* Baltimore: Johns Hopkins University Press, 2002.
> A collection of papers on aspects of Edison's laboratory and how it went about the process of invention.

Smart, James R. *"A Wonderful Invention": A Brief History of the Phonograph from Tinfoil to the LP.* Washington, D.C.: Library of Congress, 1977.
> An illustrated account of early developments in the phonograph.

Article

Briggs, John. "[Interview with] Reese Jenkins: Edison's Archives." *Omni,* April 1989, pp. 82–87, 102–110.
> A researcher reveals surprising details about how Thomas Edison's mind worked.

Web Sites

Dirks, Tim. "Film History by Decade." Available online. URL: http://www.filmsite.org/filmh.html. Accessed on February 8, 2006.
> Provides a clickable time line by decade for a detailed history of the movies.

Schoenherr, Steve. "Recording Technology History." Available online. URL: http://history.acusd.edu/gen/recording/notes.html. Accessed on February 8, 2006.
> Includes many historical images relating to the development of different forms of recording from cylinder to CD, including devices such as microphones and speakers.

"Thomas Edison National Historical Site." National Park Service. Available online. URL: http://www.nps.gov/edis/home.htm. Accessed on February 8, 2006.
> Introduces and provides resources relating to Edison's work and to the restoration and renovation of Edison's home and laboratory.

4

INTO THE ETHER

GUGLIELMO MARCONI AND WIRELESS TELEGRAPHY

The 19th-century communications technology of the telegraph and telephone is based on one idea: the ability to change electricity and magnetism into each other. Starting with the simple on/off signaling of the telegraph, inventors gradually learned how to use a continuous electric current to carry the complex pattern of the human voice, creating the telephone. As the century drew toward an end, however, a new understanding of the nature of electricity offered the possibility of communication without wires.

Discovering Radio Waves

In 1864, physicist James Clerk Maxwell published a new theory of electromagnetism. Unlike Hans Christian Ørsted, Michael Faraday, and earlier experimenters, Maxwell took a comprehensive mathematical approach. He devised a set of equations that explained the shape of electromagnetic fields and how electricity and magnetism interacted with each other. Maxwell's theory implied that any change in an electrical or magnetic field starts a train of waves that radiate into space. Further, he suggested that these "electromagnetic waves" traveled at exactly the same speed as light, about 186,000 miles (300,000 km) per second. In fact, Maxwell suggested, the only difference between light and electricity was in the length of the waves.

Guglielmo Marconi built a practical wireless telegraph system that provided life-saving communications for ships and competition for the Atlantic telegraph cable business. (Smithsonian Institution Photo No. 52202)

Scientists argued about whether Maxwell's bold hypothesis was correct. In 1879, the Berlin Academy of Science offered a prize to anyone who could prove that electromagnetic waves existed. The challenge was taken up by German physicist Heinrich Hertz (1857–94), who in 1887 devised a simple experiment. He fed current from a battery into a wire coil that was placed near a second coil that was more tightly wound. Following the laws of electromagnetism, the current in the first coil induced a rapidly oscillating current in the second coil. The current was then led to a pair of capacitors—metal plates that stored the current until they could hold no more. At that point, the plates discharged, sending a spark across the space between two small, ball-shaped electrodes.

Hertz then built a simple detector that used a wire with a ball on either end, bent into a circle so that the ends were not quite touching. He found that when a current was discharged in the main apparatus while the detector was held some distance away, a smaller spark leapt across the detector's gap. This showed that electromagnetic waves were being transmitted through the air by the oscillating current and received by the detector. Maxwell's theory had been proven correct.

In 1892, British scientist Sir William Crookes wrote an article titled "Some Possibilities of Electricity." Among them, as quoted by author Steven Lubar, was

> *the bewildering possibility of telegraphy without wires. . . . Any two friends, having first decided on their special wavelength and attuned their respective instruments to mutual receptivity could thus communicate as long and as often as they pleased by timing the impulses to produce the long and short intervals in the ordinary Morse code.*

Another distinguished scientist, Oliver Lodge (also quoted by Lubar), agreed that wireless telegraphy was possible. But at the

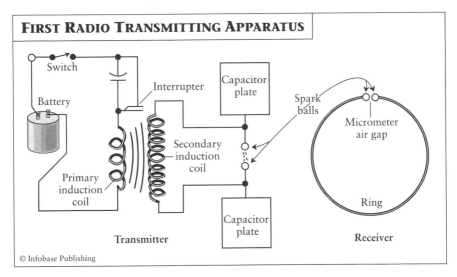

FIRST RADIO TRANSMITTING APPARATUS

© Infobase Publishing

Heinrich Hertz built a simple circuit to test James Clerk Maxwell's electromagnetic wave theory. The current from the battery is raised to a high voltage as it passes between the primary and secondary coils. A spark then jumps between the ball-shaped electrodes and generates radio waves that can be detected as a small spark passing between the ends of the wire hoop in the receiver.

time, he did not think there was much point to it. Why bother, Lodge asked

thus with difficulty [to] telegraph . . . across space instead of with ease by the highly developed and simple telegraphic and telephonic methods rendered possible with the use of a connecting wire?

Within a decade, these questions would be answered.

OTHER INVENTORS: FORGOTTEN RADIO EXPERIMENTERS

Wireless telegraphy was almost literally "in the air" by the end of the 19th century. With six decades of telegraphy behind them, it was not much of a stretch for experimenters of the era to realize that any new electrical phenomena that could be produced in pulses could be used to signal messages. Indeed, "induction telegraphs" were already on use on some railroads, allowing moving trains to communicate over regular telegraph lines by using induced current to carry the message the few inches between train and wire.

Back in 1865, West Virginia dentist Mahlon Loomis apparently transmitted wireless messages between two Virginia mountaintops 14 miles (23 km) apart, using kites. In 1870, he sent signals between two ships two miles apart on Chesapeake Bay. It is not clear how his apparatus worked, but it may have relied on transmitting current through the earth or water itself.

In 1885, Thomas Edison built a "grasshopper telegraph" that performed a similar function to Hertz's apparatus, transmitting a spark across a gap between train and receiver. Edison even patented the receiving antenna—a patent Marconi later had to ask to use.

While Marconi was beginning his own wireless experiments, a Russian inventor named Alexander Stepanovitch Popov was sending signals up to 820 feet (250 m) at St. Petersburg University. Popov did not patent or commercially develop his invention, however.

Marconi and Wireless Telegraphy

The person who would first turn "Hertz waves" into a practical, commercial technology was a young Italian named Guglielmo Marconi. Marconi was born on April 25, 1874, in Bologna, Italy, and at age 20, he was still living with his mother in their Italian villa and looking for a way to make a successful career.

Marconi was similar to Samuel Morse in some ways. Both were imaginative, rather dreamy persons who decided to become inventors because they felt their careers had stalled and that it was worth taking a chance on something new. Both were interested in making money, not in scientific discoveries. While Marconi described himself as "an ardent amateur student of electricity," like Morse, he had little mechanical skill and would depend on finding good assistants who could make his ideas work. But Marconi, even more so than Morse, had the persistence and showmanship that helped 19th-century inventors turn their ideas into industries.

Marconi began by building an apparatus similar to the one Hertz had used to prove the existence of radio waves. He added a telegraph key to the spark generator so he could send the dots and dashes of Morse code. It worked as expected but was not really a practical communications device. When he moved the device outdoors to try for longer-range transmissions, Marconi made a lucky discovery: When one terminal of the generator was connected to a metal pole and the other to the ground, the invisible waves traveled much further.

Hertz had detected radio waves at close range by the spark they created in the receiving antenna. This was fine for proving that the waves existed, but it worked only at short distances. Marconi needed a detector that responded to radio waves at a distance.

Back in 1866, an English engineer had noticed that when lightning struck a tube filled with iron filings, its normal high resistance to electricity fell abruptly. Telegraph builders began to add such tubes to their circuits to help protect them from lightning by discharging it into the ground. A number of scientists also observed this effect but did not find it remarkable until 1894, when Oliver Lodge suggested that the tube might be detecting electromagnetic waves from the lightning.

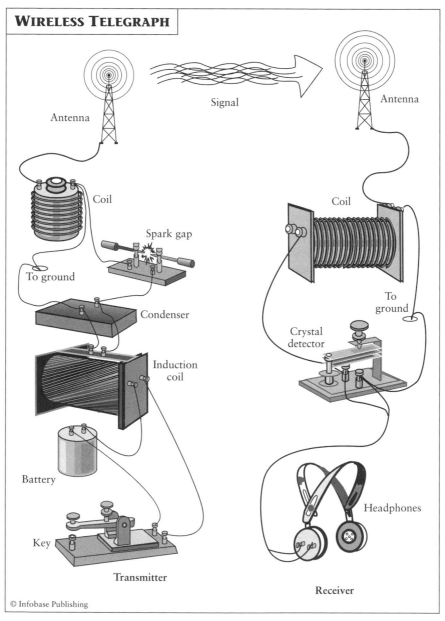

WIRELESS TELEGRAPH

Antenna

Signal

Antenna

Coil

Coil

Spark gap

To ground

To ground

Condenser

Crystal detector

Induction coil

Battery

Headphones

Key

Transmitter

Receiver

© Infobase Publishing

The wireless telegraph essentially combines a traditional telegraph key with a circuit similar to the one used in Hertz's experiment. Later, simple detectors using metal filings or crystals were replaced by far more sensitive vacuum tubes.

Marconi learned about this tube, now called a "coherer," and decided to use it as a detector for wireless telegraph signals. Like Edison, Marconi believed in systematically trying every variation of a device he could think of, in the hope of improving it. Marconi eventually discovered that a mixture of nickel and silver filings worked better than iron did.

Building an Industry

Gradually, Marconi extended the range of his transmitter to several miles. When the Italian government refused to buy rights to his invention, he decided to go to England and patent it there. Why England? For one thing, Marconi's mother's family lived there and was willing to help fund his experiments. But a more important reason was that there was an application where wireless did not have to compete with the wire telegraph: communication between ships, or between ship and shore. At the time, England was the world's foremost maritime nation and had the greatest need for this kind of communication.

William H. Preece, the head engineer of the British Post Office, had been unsuccessfully experimenting with wireless telegraphy with the same application in mind. When Marconi demonstrated his apparatus to him on Salisbury Plain and out in the English Channel, Preece was very impressed.

British investors also proved to be interested in the possibilities of Marconi's invention. On June 20, 1897, the Marconi Wireless Telegraph Company was founded. One of its first customers was the famous insurance company Lloyd's of London, which installed a wireless link so that an offshore lighthouse could report arriving ships.

Marconi's company, like Bell Telephone, decided to lease rather than sell its equipment. This prevented the British government from taking over the wireless service as it had with the telegraph and telephone. It also meant that Marconi would be able to control maritime communications for a decade or more, since he could specify that Marconi's operators would communicate only with other Marconi installations.

Marconi tirelessly publicized the wireless. In 1899, he went to the United States, which had defeated the Spanish in a short war and was beginning to think of itself as a world power. Americans were also ready to cheer on their entry in the International Yacht Races. The *New York Herald* announced in a front-page headline: "Marconi Will Report the Yacht Races by His Wireless System." Many Americans therefore read about the wireless for the first time and were eager to learn more.

As Susan Douglas recounts in *Inventing American Broadcasting,* Marconi later recalled that

> *what impressed the public most was the extraordinary rapidity of the system. Whenever the Marconi bulletins, as they were called, were posted all over the city, the public was less than seventy-five seconds behind the yachts and in many cases less than thirty seconds.*

Finer Tuning

As more experimenters went on the air with their own wireless systems, a new problem arose—interference. In the 1901 yacht races, Marconi's and Lee De Forest's competing installations often drowned each other out. They had to agree to take turns transmitting, and, meanwhile, a third transmitter, operated by a company seeking to make money on the stock market, interfered with both of them. The magazine *Electrical World* noted that "the problem of securing immunity from interference remains to be solved."

The problem was that there was no easy way to tune the early transmitters and receivers so they could connect on a particular frequency. In 1897, Oliver Lodge discovered "syntony," the fact that each electrical circuit has a particular frequency at which the entire circuit resonates, or vibrates together, using energy more efficiently. Marconi used this idea to develop tuning mechanisms that could change the resonance. If two wireless installations tuned to the same resonance, they would receive much less interference from other signals.

There was still a problem with the detector, though. The coherer had a mechanism that used a hammer to tap the metal filings loose

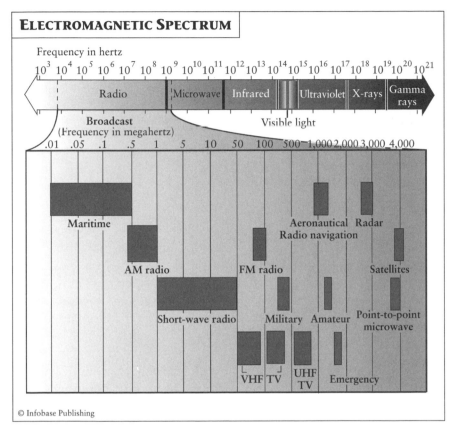

Different frequency ranges of the broadcast spectrum are allocated to different kinds of radio and television services. Note that as the frequency increases, microwaves gradually give way to infrared light and then visible light.

after each signal was received, preparing it to respond to the next signal. This made for a slow rate of reception.

In 1895, another great British physicist, Ernest Rutherford, had reported that electromagnetic waves tended to demagnetize magnetic objects. Rutherford suggested that magnetism might be used to detect "Hertzian" (radio) waves. In 1902, Marconi patented a new detector based on this principle. It used a moving band of wire that passed continuously between two horseshoe magnets. Normally, a given section of the wire kept its magnetism for some time as it passed away from the magnet. But when radio waves hit the wire, it lost its magnetism. This change of magnetism caused a current that could be turned into a signal that the wireless operator could hear. This new "maggie" detector was more sensitive and reliable than the older coherer mechanism. Yet again, Marconi showed that he could "borrow" a brand-new scientific idea and use it to build an improvement in his apparatus.

Leaping the Atlantic

Marconi had successfully demonstrated his wireless equipment over relatively short distances. He now decided to send signals more than 2,000 miles (3200 km) across the Atlantic Ocean. Many scientists doubted that any wireless signal, no matter how powerful, could travel for thousands of miles. They believed that electromagnetic waves always travelled in straight lines. The waves would therefore not follow the curvature of the earth but rather beam out into space and be lost.

Marconi had little interest in the scientific debate. He began to build a transmitting station at Poldhu, a bay in Cornwall, in the southwestern part of Great Britain. Marconi's antenna was a veritable Stonehenge, consisting of a ring of 20 wooden masts, each about 200 feet (60 m) high, arranged in a circle 200 feet (60 m) in diameter, and covering about an acre (0.40 ha) in area. Altogether, about 4,000 wires were strung from the masts. Marconi built a similar giant antenna array at Cape Cod, Massachusetts.

Marconi tried to make his transmitter as powerful as possible. As *McClure's Magazine* observed: "When the operator pressed the telegraphic key, a spark a foot long and as thick as a man's wrist, the most powerful electric flash yet devised, sprang across the gap; the very ground nearby quivered and crackled with the energy."

The testing began, but within a month, fierce storms had demolished both antennae. Marconi had hoped to start right away with a complete two-way transatlantic service. Now, his business devastated by the loss, Marconi struggled to find a way just to get a simple signal across the ocean to show that it could be done. He set up a simpler antenna at Poldhu and moved his receiving station to Newfoundland, which was considerably closer to England. He would gain height for his receiving antenna by attaching a kite to it.

On December 15, 1901, newspaper headlines announced that Marconi had heard in Newfoundland a message sent by his station in Britain. The message was simply the "dot dot dot" that stands for the letter S in Morse code. Although there was later some controversy over whether a signal had been successfully received, it soon became clear that truly long-distance wireless communication was possible after all.

Marconi's feat excited the imagination of many writers. Ray Stannard Baker, writing for *McClure's Magazine*, asked his readers to

Think for a moment of sitting here on the edge of North America and listening to communication sent through space across nearly 2,000 miles of ocean from the edge of Europe! A cable, marvelous as it is, maintains a tangible and material connection between

---

SOLVING PROBLEMS: LONG-DISTANCE RADIO

It turned out that scientists were right that radio waves basically travel in straight lines. After Marconi's successful long-distance transmission, British physicist Oliver Heaviside (1850–1925) and American electrical engineer Arthur Edwin Kennelly (1861–1949) theorized that there was a layer of the upper atmosphere that was electrically charged and that acted like a mirror to bounce radio signals back down to earth hundreds or thousands of miles from their origin. This layer came to be known as the ionosphere.

The ionosphere varies in height from 50 to 240 miles (80 to 385 km). If a listener turns the tuning dial of an AM radio slowly during the late hours of night, it is possible to pick up stations from hundreds of miles away. That is because at night part of the ionosphere layer is in a higher, thinner part of the atmosphere, and it lets radio signals bounce back to earth instead of being absorbed in the air. Indeed, distance listening, or "DXing," is a popular pastime for radio amateurs.

speaker and hearer; one can grasp its meaning. But here is nothing but space, a pole with a pendant [dangling] wire on one side of a broad, curving ocean, an uncertain kite struggling in the air on the other—and thought passing between.

Growing the Wireless Business

While ship-based communications was a natural "fit" for Marconi's wireless business, the much-larger market for international communications was already being served by the transoceanic cables operated by companies such as Western Union. Cable capacity had fallen behind the growing demand, but the operators had a virtual monopoly and felt little pressure to change. As the *New York Times* (quoted by Susan Douglas in *Inventing American Broadcasting*) complained:

There has been no reduction in the cost to the public of cable communication for the past score [20] of years. This has not only been a distinct hindrance to the development of business, but it has been a hindrance to the improvement of relations of nations to each other. The cable companies have been as incapable of improvement as the Martian canals, and were managed with about as much reference to the needs and wishes of the population on earth.

The *Times* hoped that Marconi's wireless would offer a cheaper alternative. A pair of wireless stations was much less expensive and much easier to install than a new Atlantic cable. But it would take considerable technical effort to make wireless truly reliable over long distances. Marconi and his backers needed to make money soon and that meant ship-to-ship and ship-to-shore communication. That was something they could handle with existing equipment and without competition from cables.

The most dramatic use of wireless was for rescuing ships in trouble at sea. During the night of January 23, 1909, the lookout on the steamship *Republic* heard the blasts of a horn and saw a huge shape looming out of the darkness. It was too late to avoid a collision, and the *Republic* crashed into another steamer, the *Florida*. Fortunately, the *Republic*'s wireless operator and his equipment were not hurt. He began to send the letters CQD, the distress call that was eventually replaced by the now familiar SOS. He was able to give his ship's approximate position.

Several wireless-equipped ships responded to the distress call. As the *Republic* began to sink, passengers and crew calmly got into the lifeboats. The ship *Baltic* was the first rescuer on the scene. Its wireless operator sent a running account of the rescue operations:

> *The steamship* Florida *collided with the* Republic *175 miles east of the Ambrose Lightship at 5:30* A.M. *on Saturday. The* Republic's *passengers were transferred to the* Florida. *The* Republic *is rapidly sinking. It is doubtful if she will remain afloat much longer. The* Baltic *has taken all the passengers aboard . . .*

Later, the operator reported, "I can send no more. I have been constantly at the key without sleep for fifty-two hours."

After wireless had so dramatically proved its value, the United States and most other seafaring nations passed laws requiring that ships carry wireless equipment.

A Voice in the Air

On Christmas Eve of 1906, wireless operators aboard ships off the New England coast put on their headsets and waited for a special message they had been told to expect from a station operated by Reginald Fessenden (1866–1932), a Canadian-born physicist and electrical engineer.

Most of them no doubt were expecting some sort of Christmas greeting encoded in the usual Morse dots and dashes. Instead, they heard Fessenden's voice, music from phonograph records, and even a bit of violin music played "live" by the inventor!

About six years earlier, Fessenden had begun to create a radio system that could transmit the human voice—what would become known as radio telephony. To do this, he had to make several changes in the wireless technology of the time.

Regular radio telegraphy, like its wire-carried counterpart, uses small bursts of current. These bursts can carry the simple dots and dashes of Morse code, but Fessenden realized that to carry sound, a continuous signal would have to be generated. The signal would have the pattern of the waves of voice or music superimposed on it—what is called "modulation."

In order to carry the detailed pattern of sound, the current would have to have a much higher frequency, or number, of waves generated per second. To generate these high-frequency waves, Fessenden needed varying or "alternating" current. Existing generators (alternators) normally produced current at the rate of 60 cycles per second (which is still the U.S. standard for electric power today.) Fessenden needed an alternator that would produce tens of thousands of cycles per second. When he went to General Electric and insisted they build him such a machine, they decided to meet the challenge, and newly employed Ernst Alexanderson was given the job.

Alexanderson came through and eventually delivered a machine that could run at 50,000 cycles. With this machine, Fessenden was able to generate a continuous radio wave and create the voice-carrying radio telephone. Thanks to Fessenden, the United States entered World War I with the world's most powerful radio transmitters.

Fessenden thought of his invention as simply doing for wireless what the telephone did for the telegraph—making "point-to-point" voice communication possible. (In a way, therefore, Fessenden did for Marconi what Bell had done for Morse.) It did not occur to Fessenden that there might be a reason to regularly send speech and music over the airwaves to a whole audience of listeners. This idea, radio broadcasting, would create a new revolution in communications (see chapter 5, "Triumph and Tragedy").

Marconi, meanwhile, became an international celebrity. He served as an officer in the Italian army in World War I, and then as a diplomat. During the 1920s, Marconi continued his research, developing the "beam system" for coordinating international short-wave communication. He also studied very short waves (microwaves) and even demonstrated what would later come to be known as radar. Both the Italian and British governments bestowed honors on him. Marconi died in Rome on July 20, 1937.

Chronology

1864	James Clerk Maxwell develops the theory of electromagnetic waves
1874	Guglielmo Marconi is born on April 25 in Bologna, Italy
1887	Heinrich Hertz first sends and receives radio waves
1895	Marconi begins experimenting with "Hertzian" waves
1896	Marconi arrives in England; he demonstrates and patents wireless radio communication
1897	The Marconi Wireless Telegraph Company is founded
1899	Marconi reports international yacht races from a wireless equipped boat
1901	Marconi sends the Morse letter S across the Atlantic from Britain to Newfoundland
1906	Reginald Fessenden broadcasts voice and music to astonished wireless operators
1909	First use of wireless to rescue a ship (the steamer *Republic*) at sea
1912	United States begins to regulate wireless to prevent interference problems
1920s	Marconi, now a celebrity, continues research with short-wave and microwave radio
1937	Marconi dies on July 20 in Rome

Further Reading

Books

Douglas, Susan J. *Inventing American Broadcasting, 1899–1922.* Baltimore: Johns Hopkins University Press, 1987.
> Describes the technical and business developments in wireless telegraphy and early broadcast radio, as well as the social context.

Dunlap, Orrin E. *Marconi: The Man and His Wireless.* New York: Macmillan, 1937.
> An older but still informative biography of Marconi.

Leinwoll, Stanley. *From Spark to Satellite: A History of Radio Communication.* New York: Charles Scribner's Sons, 1979.
> A good, comprehensive survey of the development of radio.

Lubar, Stephen. *InfoCulture: The Smithsonian Book of Information Age Inventions.* Boston: Houghton Mifflin, 1993.
> Includes material on radio technology and broadcasting.

Parker, Steve. *Guglielmo Marconi & Radio.* Broomall, Pa.: Chelsea House Publishers, 1995.
> Biography of Marconi for young readers.

Web Sites

"United States Early Radio History." Available online. URL: http://earlyradiohistory.us. Accessed on February 8, 2006.
> Provides overviews and fascinating documents relating to early experiments in radio transmission, radio telegraphy, and early broadcasting.

"U.S. Marconi Museum." Guglielmo Marconi Foundation. Available online. URL: http://www.marconiusa.org. Accessed on August 28, 2006.
> Describes a museum in New Bedford, Connecticut, devoted to Marconi and his work.

5

TRIUMPH AND TRAGEDY

EDWIN ARMSTRONG AND RADIO BROADCASTING

In 1915, David Sarnoff, chief inspector for the Marconi Wireless Telegraph Company of America, wrote a memo in which he proposed a new kind of radio service "which would make radio a 'household utility' in the same sense as the piano or phonograph." He called the new device a "radio music box" and explained that "the receiver could be arranged for several different wavelengths, which should be changeable with the throwing of a single switch or the pressing of a single button." Sarnoff went on to note that radio listeners could be provided with baseball games, news reports, and musical concerts. Sarnoff's memo fell on deaf ears, however. To the Marconi Company, radio was simply wireless telegraphy.

Edwin Armstrong developed key radio inventions, including feedback amplification and the superheterodyne. He wanted to replace static-plagued AM radio with his new FM system, but RCA had other plans. (Photo courtesy of Jeanne Hammond)

The development of radio broadcasting would demand new ideas in both technology and business. An inventor named Edwin Armstrong would make many of the key discoveries that make modern radio possible. In the end, however, Armstrong would become the victim of social change as corporate power overshadowed the individual inventor.

The Birth of Electronics

So far, wireless technology had depended on relatively simple electromechanical devices. The signal was generated by a spark or by a spinning generator, or alternator. The signal was detected by a

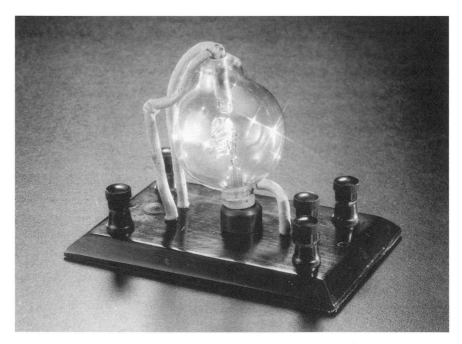

Thomas Edison built this tube to demonstrate the "Edison effect"—a mysterious flow of current in a lightbulb. Although Edison patented the device, he did not really understand what was going on—that would require the discovery of the electron at the end of the 19th century. (Smithsonian Institution, Photo No. 89-19702)

coherer, magnetic detector, or other device that responded to the effects of the waves.

The first clue to a new way to generate and detect radio waves had come in 1882, barely a few years after Heinrich Hertz had first detected radio waves. Thomas Edison was trying to figure out why his lightbulbs began to blacken and burn out sooner than expected. Edison discovered that a small electric current was flowing inside the bulb, traveling through the vacuum and depositing particles from the carbon filament on the inside of the glass. Edison thought of a way to solve the problem. He put a small piece of tinfoil on the inside of the bulb and connected it to a positively charged plate, diverting the current.

Edison had little understanding of this mysterious current and not much curiosity about it. In 1897, however, British physicist Joseph J. Thomson had been studying the flow of electricity in gases. He discovered that the "rays" that a hot filament, or "cathode," gave off could be bent by magnetic and electrical fields. Thomson concluded that what had appeared to be some kind of radiation was in fact a stream of negatively charged particles many times smaller than an atom. He called these particles "electrons."

In 1904, another researcher, John Fleming, was working for Guglielmo Marconi, who wanted him to come up with a new detector for wireless waves. Years earlier, Fleming had worked for Thomas Edison, and he remembered the mysterious current in the lightbulbs. Fleming wondered whether he could turn a lightbulb into a radio detector. He inserted a piece of tinfoil inside the bulb and connected it to a galvanometer (current detector), a coil, and then to the negative power terminal. When he turned on a wireless transmitter, the galvanometer showed that a current was flowing in the coil.

The current alternated (changed directions and charge) at the same rate as the frequency of the transmitter. When the current was positive, it flowed toward the negatively charged filament. When the current's charge changed to negative, it was repelled by the negative filament and stopped flowing. This meant that the alternating current from the radio signal was being turned into a one-way, or direct current. This process is called rectification. It also meant that Fleming now had a radio-wave detector that was more reliable than any that depended on a mechanical magnetic device. Because

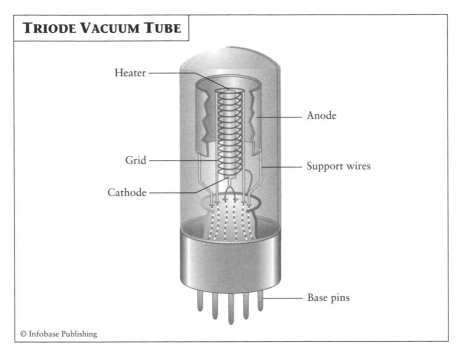

TRIODE VACUUM TUBE

Heater

Anode

Grid

Support wires

Cathode

Base pins

© Infobase Publishing

The diode and triode vacuum tubes have a cathode that releases electrons and is surrounded by an anode. When the anode is positive, the negatively charged electrons flow toward it. If the anode current is negative, it will repel (and block) the electrons. The back-and-forth alternating current is thus converted to a one-directional direct current. The triode adds a grid with a separate, more powerful current that can be varied with the signal to amplify it.

Fleming's "valve" worked by directly changing the flow of electrons, it was the first *electronic* device.

Electronic Amplification

Lee De Forest, an engineer for Western Electric, had been trying to launch his own career as an inventor. De Forest started by building a tube similar to Fleming's, but then he had an insight, as quoted by Stanley Leinwoll in *From Spark to Satellite*. De Forest realized that *[a] third, or control electrode could be located more efficiently between the wing [plate] and filament ... I decided that the interposed third electrode would be better in the form of a grid, a simple piece of wire I bent back and forth and located as close to the filament as possible.*

A small negative charge on the grid could stop the flow of electrons from the filament, or cathode, to the positive plate, or anode. A positive charge let the current flow again. Since the current being created by the radio signal consisted of alternating positive and negative

OTHER INVENTORS: THE TUMULTUOUS DE FORESTS

Iowa-born Lee De Forest (1873–1961) combined a deep interest in the mysteries of wireless with grandiose ideas about becoming an inventor of great stature and the founder of an industry. Although he filed more than 300 patents, the audion, or amplifying vacuum tube, was his main invention of lasting significance.

While De Forest's work brought him considerable financial success at first, his energy became increasingly tied up in long patent battles, particularly with Edwin Armstrong. Crooked business partners destroyed many of De Forest's business ventures, and his later attempts to develop a sound film system and a combination movie and television system met with little success.

A lesser-known aspect of De Forest's story involves his wife, Nora Stanton Blatch. A descendant of the famous women's rights pioneer Elizabeth Cady Stanton, Blatch's own independent-mindedness can be seen in her becoming the first woman to receive a civil engineering degree from Cornell University.

Blatch's engineering background and knowledge of wireless technology, as well as her business connections, made her a good working partner for De Forest. Unfortunately, she was soon relegated to a domestic role and denied the opportunity to pursue her own technical interests. When the De Forest Company collapsed among charges of fraud, Blatch sued for divorce.

charges, that meant that a tiny radio signal could control the flow of a much-larger current in the grid. This imposed the wave pattern of the radio signal on the grid current, which is the equivalent of greatly strengthening, or amplifying, the signal.

De Forest patented his "audion" tube in 1906. It soon found its use in telegraph and telephone amplifiers, as well as radio.

Armstrong Gives Radio a Boost

About the time De Forest was inventing the amplifying tube, a teenage boy named Edwin Armstrong was reading about the excitement of invention. Armstrong's mother was a former schoolteacher and his father a publishing executive. Books were thus no strangers to the young boy, who was born on December 18, 1890, and grew up in New York City. The books he liked the best were such titles as *The Boy's Book of Inventions* and *Stories of the Wonders of Modern Science.* There, Armstrong could study diagrams that explained such marvels as the submarine, phonograph, and X-ray machine. When he turned to the chapter on Marconi and wireless, young Armstrong decided that was the area where he would seek inventions of his own.

Armstrong turned an attic room in the family's large Victorian house into a radio station, exchanging messages with other radio-minded boys in the neighborhood. After graduating from high school, Armstrong entered the engineering school at Columbia University, where he excelled in a rigorous series of courses in basic science and electrical engineering. Armstrong also enjoyed sports and extracurricular activities, though not when they interfered with his single-minded pursuit of radio.

By 1912, Armstrong was beginning his senior year at Columbia and had become interested in vacuum tubes. Armstrong, unlike De Forest, fully grasped the implications of the electron. He realized that because the audion tube created a steadily swinging, or oscillating, flow of electrons that moved at the speed of light, this flow could be fed back into the grid over and over again. Each time the current was fed back, it would become stronger, in effect amplifying itself more and more. Further, Armstrong tied the current flowing through the antenna (from the incoming signal) into the circuit going through the grid, making the receiver even more sensitive.

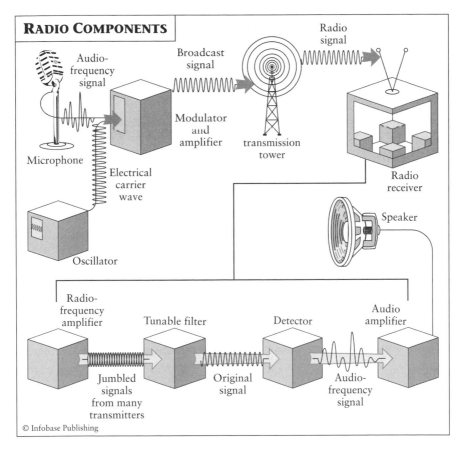

RADIO COMPONENTS

Radio
signal

Audio-
frequency
signal

Broadcast
signal

Modulator
and
amplifier

transmission
tower

Microphone

Electrical
carrier
wave

Radio
receiver

Oscillator

Speaker

Radio-
frequency
amplifier

Tunable filter

Detector

Audio
amplifier

Jumbled
signals
from many
transmitters

Original
signal

Audio-
frequency
signal

© Infobase Publishing

Modern radios have several circuits for processing a signal, including detectors, filters, and amplifiers.

The result of Armstrong's "regeneration" circuit was a dramatic improvement in radio reception. Armstrong also discovered that if he fed the current back through the circuit enough times, the tube began to give off radio waves of its own. This meant that electronic radio transmitters were also possible.

When the United States entered World War I in 1917, Armstrong joined the army and went to France. During the war, Armstrong developed powerful radio transmitters and receivers for field head-quarters and trenches, and he also pioneered in equipping airplanes with radio sets.

SOCIAL IMPACT: EMERGENCE OF TECHNICAL CULTURES

In 1907, the *New York Times Magazine* featured an article on the young men who had become "wireless wizards." These amateur wireless operators had built their own stations and spent the nights picking up messages hundreds of miles away and comparing notes with their peers. Amateur operators ("hams" for short) would make many technical contributions, particularly in pioneering the use of the short-wave frequencies. Ironically, once they had demonstrated the usefulness of a frequency band, the government would usually "kick them upstairs" to a higher frequency, turning their old haunts over to commercial broadcasters.

Young radio experimenters such as Edwin Armstrong, like the young telegraphers of Thomas Edison's youth, formed what can be called specialized cultures (or subcultures). Such groups are held together by common knowledge and preoccupations, as well as through the use of a highly technical knowledge that is opaque to outsiders.

Amateur radio would help create another enduring subculture. Hugo Gernsback, editor of *Modern Electrics,* pioneered magazine science fiction in the 1920s and helped create a legion of fans who would avidly discuss their favorite authors.

The amateur radio culture and the early science-fiction fan culture were almost completely male pursuits. The computer "hacker" culture that emerged in the late 1950s and early 1960s would be mainly male too. But the wider Internet culture that emerged in the mid-1990s would benefit from a growing number of young women who were comfortable with technology and who viewed it as being as much their birthright as that of any boy.

Broadcasting Begins

After the war, Armstrong and other pioneers finally brought radio into the electronic age. With vacuum tube amplifiers and transmitters, radio became reliable enough to become a consumer product. In 1920, Armstrong announced a new invention that came from his wartime work with high-frequency radio: the "superheterodyne" circuit. The superheterodyne worked by generating a radio frequency that was close to (but not the same as) that of the incoming signal and by electronically combining the two somewhat in the way two piano keys can be pressed at the same time to produce a third sound. Because a combined signal has a frequency that is the difference between the original signal and the second signal, the resulting signal was at a much lower frequency and easier to work with. The new signal could then be passed through one or more stages of amplification. The receiver no longer had to "stretch" to fit the signal: The signal could in effect be adjusted to the range where the amplifiers worked most efficiently. As the 1920s began, many amateur radio operators bought the new equipment and set up their own broadcast stations, carrying music and news to their local community.

The Westinghouse Corporation then built what many consider to be the first commercial radio station, KDKA in Pittsburgh, Pennsylvania. On November 2, 1920, the station began broadcasting the returns of the presidential election in which Warren G. Harding beat James W. Cox. Radio as we know it today had arrived.

TRENDS: A "SNAPSHOT" OF THE RADIO INDUSTRY IN THE UNITED STATES, 1923

In his book *Empire of the Air,* author Tom Lewis assembles some facts and figures to show how the radio broadcast industry in the United States, in its first three years, mushroomed:

Number of stations: 1920 (1); 1922 (30); 1923 (556)
State with the most stations in 1923: California (63)
Number of radio sets produced: 1922 (100,000); 1923 (500,000)
Cost of a "complete tube [radio] set" from Sears Roebuck in 1923: $23.50
Mix of programming from radio station WJZ in 1923: "98 baritone solos, 6 baseball games, 3 boxing bouts, 67 church services, 7 football games, 10 harmonica solos, 74 organ concerts, 340 soprano recitals, 40 plays, 723 talks and lectures, and 205 bedtime stories."

As the 20th century went on, the radio became the "entertainment center" in many homes. (Library of Congress)

As J. Fred MacDonald notes in his broadcasting history *Don't Touch That Dial!:*

> *Radio aerials now began to clutter the skyline, and people shopping for new homes began looking for locales with good reception. Since early 1922, a daily radio log listing programs for the day became a regular feature of most newspapers, and by the end of the year twenty-seven [radio] fan magazines were being published in the United States. . . .*

But who was going to pay for radio broadcasting, and who would control what went on the air? In Great Britain and many

other European countries, the government controlled the broadcast networks just as they had the telegraph and telephone. The
radio listener usually paid the government an annual fee for each
radio set.

In the United States, there was no tradition of government owner-
ship of communications. Stations were private businesses that sold
advertising time to sponsors, making radio free for the listener,
though at the cost of having to listen to numerous commercials. The
government served more as a "traffic cop" that gave out licenses to
stations and tried to keep them from interfering with each others'
transmissions.

Creating the Programming

Besides paying for radio, there was the question of what kinds of
programs were to be broadcast. Playing recordings of popular and
classical music was certainly a possibility, although musicians'
unions and record companies tried at first to stop radio from giving out their product for free. (Eventually, a system was devised by
which the record companies and musicians would receive a payment
every time a song was played on the air.)

Spoken drama was another popular choice. At first, according to
radio writer Arch Oboler:

> *Radio in those days was an imitation of motion pictures, and an
> echo of the stage. No one had really used it as a theater of the mind,
> had realized that a few words, a sound effect, a bit of music, could
> transport—in the mind of the listeners—one to any corner of the
> world, evoke emotions that were deep in the consciousness of the
> listener.*

But radio soon evolved unique forms of drama or changed existing ones to fit its format: the detective story, the western adventure
story, the science-fiction superhero, and the soap opera—the last
so named because it was aimed mainly at housewives and featured
commercials for laundry soap.

Radio's Social Impact

A severe economic depression brought social turmoil to the United States and much of the industrialized world during the 1930s. As people looked to leaders for assurance, radio became a powerful political force. Beginning on March 12, 1933, President Franklin D. Roosevelt began to speak directly to the American people on his radio "fireside chats."

Leaders have always used their speaking skills to persuade people, of course. The difference was that radio made it possible for the first time to "personally" persuade millions of people at the same time. Whether the leader spoke from the fireside or took on the more sinister tones of Germany's Adolf Hitler or the USSR's Joseph Stalin, the power of the new medium could not be denied. As the world lurched toward a devastating new war, radio newscasters such as Edward R. Murrow brought the latest developments from Europe directly to American homes.

When, in 1938, a "news broadcast" by Orson Welles claimed that Martians were invading the world and destroying whole armies with disintegrator beams, many listeners believed what they were hearing and panicked. They had learned to rely on the radio for information and assurance as well as entertainment.

Battle in the Courts

With his inventions being fundamental to the development of the radio industry, Edwin Armstrong might well have expected that his career would follow the path set by Bell, Edison, and Marconi—bringing not only financial success but also the ability to shape a new industry.

The American Marconi Company had agreed to pay Armstrong for the use of his regeneration circuit, but AT&T, the huge telephone company, said that it could use it without payment because someone else had invented it. Armstrong became embroiled in what would become the first of many debilitating legal battles when several inventors indeed claimed that they had discovered regeneration first.

Of these rivals, the most persistent was Lee De Forest. When he discovered Armstrong's patent, De Forest filed one of his own, together with a complicated and confusing explanation and a circuit diagram. The patent examiner rejected it because he saw that De Forest's circuit was fundamentally the same as Armstrong's already-patented one.

De Forest did not give up, however, and the battle moved from court to court. Armstrong had neglected to mention the transmitting feature of the circuit in his original patent, but De Forest did include it in his rival patent, somewhat strengthening his claim. Nevertheless, court after court rejected De Forest's claim and awarded patent rights to Armstrong.

But then Armstrong made a mistake. He had been deeply angered by De Forest's persistence in claiming an invention that nearly all electrical engineers had agreed was Armstrong's original idea. When De Forest continued to use the invention without payment, an outraged Armstrong went on the offensive and filed suit against De Forest.

At first, Armstrong again seemed to prevail in the courts, but eventually De Forest found a judge who was confused about the technical issues and decided in favor of De Forest. The case went to the U.S. Supreme Court, which simply affirmed the latest decision in De Forest's favor.

Armstrong had also suffered a personal blow. As legal costs ate away most of his savings, he had turned for financial help to his longtime friend David Sarnoff. Sarnoff, who had worked with Armstrong in the early days when radio broadcasting was only a dream, was now head of the Radio Corporation of America (RCA), the biggest company in the radio industry. But while he expressed personal sympathy, Sarnoff refused to back Armstrong. RCA had an arrangement to use De Forest's patent, and Sarnoff did not want this beneficial arrangement to be threatened.

Introducing FM

Armstrong still refused to give up. He began to work on a third great invention, frequency modulation (FM). Standard radio transmissions used amplitude modulation (AM). This meant that the sound to be broadcast was used to vary the amplitude, or strength, of the signal. The problem with AM was that any electrical discharge in the environment, such as a lightning storm or even the spark plug in a car, could affect an AM wave, causing a burst of static.

Armstrong wondered what would happen if he built a circuit that modulated the frequency rather than the amplitude. John Renshaw Carson, a researcher at Bell Laboratories, did not think much of the idea, declaring (according to the "Edwin Armstrong" Web site) that "I have proven, mathematically, that this type of modulation inherently distorts without any compensating advantages whatsoever. Static, like the poor, will always be with us."

Like Marconi, Armstrong did not think much of such expert opinion. As quoted on the Armstrong Web page, he "could never accept findings based almost exclusively on mathematics. It ain't ignorance that causes all the trouble in the world. It's the things people know that ain't so."

Armstrong was still working for RCA, but Sarnoff seemed reluctant to help him with FM. It turned out that Sarnoff was much more interested in developing television broadcasting (see chapter 6, "The Ghost Light"). He shut down Armstrong's FM lab and transmitter on the roof of the Empire State Building.

By November 5, 1935, however, Armstrong had made other arrangements. At a meeting of the Society of Radio Engineers, he gave a lecture explaining the principles of FM. He then raised the curtain, revealing what appeared to be an ordinary radio set. First, he tuned it to the regular, static-filled AM broadcast band. Armstrong then tuned it to his FM test station, and the static completely disappeared. Out of the silence came the announcer's voice, music, and sounds as delicate as the pouring of water into a glass. The audience had encountered true high-fidelity sound for the first time.

After World War II, Armstrong continued his commercial development of FM, which by then had attracted a small but enthusiastic group of stations and listeners.

Sarnoff needed to use FM for the sound portion of television. He refused to pay Armstrong to use the patent. Again, Armstrong went to court, but he was now up against the legal department of one of the world's largest corporations. A further blow came when RCA successfully urged the government to assign the original FM broadcasting frequencies to the new television service. This made all existing FM equipment obsolete and virtually bankrupted Armstrong.

The End of the Lone Inventor?

Armstrong eventually snapped under the relentless pressure. He hit his wife, Marion, shattering 30 years of happy marriage. They separated, and on January 31, 1954, he wrote the following note to her:

> *I am heartbroken because I cannot see you once again. I deeply regret what has happened between us. I cannot understand how I could hurt the dearest thing in the whole world to me. I would give my life to turn back to the time when we were so happy and free. God keep you and may the Lord have mercy on your soul.*

The next morning, Edwin Armstrong jumped out of the window of his 13th-floor apartment.

Armstrong's life and death raise important questions about the history of invention in the modern world. Author Gary Stock suggests that Armstrong

> *was among the last of the great individual American inventors, a breed presently reduced in rank or perhaps extinct, in a period during which vast corporations came to dominate virtually all scientific and technological development in this country. . . .*

Although Edwin Armstrong was no more, his widow, Marion fought tenaciously to vindicate his patent claims. In 1967, the family finally won its last suit over the FM patents, against Motorola Corporation. In the years since, Armstrong's stature as an inventor has continued to grow. He received the Medal of Honor of the Institute of Radio Engineers (1917) and the Edison Medal of the American Institute of Electrical Engineers (1942). In 1980, Armstrong was inducted into the National Inventors Hall of Fame.

SOLVING PROBLEMS: HEDY LAMARR V. THE JAMMERS

People who are always yakking on their cell phones might want to pause for a moment to think of Hedy Lamarr (1913–2000). What did the glamorous Austrian actress have to do with electronics? Quite a bit, actually. Before World War II, Lamarr was married to a German arms designer. She overheard many conversations about experiments with radio-controlled rockets and torpedoes, and evidently, she did some quiet thinking about radio on her own.

In 1942, after she had fled from the Nazis, Lamarr and music composer George Antheil patented a method for protecting radios from being jammed by enemy signals. Lamarr and Antheil's device used something called frequency hopping. The idea was to have the transmitter rapidly and unpredictably change frequency so that the jammer could not lock onto the signal. The problem was how to synchronize the transmitter and receiver so they hopped to the same frequency at the same time. Their solution: encoding the series of frequency settings on matching player piano rolls that moved at the same speed in both devices.

Today an electronic version of frequency hopping is used in cordless and cell telephones as well as global positioning satellite (GPS) systems and wireless computer networks. The technique enables many users to in effect "slice up" and share a limited number of frequencies by separating them in time.

Radio in the Modern World

Like the movies, radio responded to the challenge of television by becoming more specialized, serving in ways that were not easy for TV. By the 1960s, the big radio networks had become little more than news services. But thanks to the proliferation of local stations, radio had become the driver's companion and (thanks to the transistor) a source of portable music to take on a picnic. In the 1980s, popular "talk-radio" stations gave ordinary people a way to voice their opinions and complaints. Television had taken center stage as the great mass medium, but radio survived because it was versatile and relatively inexpensive.

Ironically, Armstrong's FM radio rose from the dead in the 1960s. Its superior sound quality made it the medium of choice for classical music, jazz, and the emerging, increasingly sophisticated sounds of rock and roll.

At the beginning of the 21st century, new flavors of radio are starting to make an impact. Whether streamed over the Internet or beamed down directly from satellites to users, new digital forms of radio provide hundreds of interference-free stations, though finding a reliable connection can sometimes be a problem.

Chronology

1882	Edison discovers a mysterious current in his lightbulbs but does not fully understand its nature
1890	Edwin Armstrong is born on December 18 in New York City
1897	Joseph J. Thomson discovers the electron
1904	John Fleming builds the first rectifying vacuum tube
1906	Lee De Forest creates the audion or triode, a vacuum tube that can amplify signals
1912	Edwin Armstrong invents the regeneration (feedback) amplifier for radio waves
1915	David Sarnoff of RCA proposes a "radio music box" for the household
1920	Armstrong invents the superheterodyne circuit used in modern radio receivers
1928	The Supreme Court upholds a court decision in favor of De Forest in a long-running patent dispute with Armstrong
1935	Armstrong stuns engineers with a demonstration of FM broadcasting

1954	Bankrupt and despondent, Armstrong commits suicide
1960s	FM radio becomes the medium of choice for music
1980s	AM "talk radio" becomes popular
2000s	Digital Internet and satellite services offer a new alternative for radio listeners

Further Reading

Books

Lessig, Lawrence. *Man of High Fidelity: Edwin Howard Armstrong.* Rev. ed. New York: Bantam Books, 1969.
> A detailed account of Armstrong's achievements and struggles, including his posthumous vindication in the courts.

Lewis, Tom. *Empire of the Air: The Men Who Made Radio.* New York: HarperCollins, 1991.
> Presents the tumultuous lives and times of radio pioneers Lee De Forest, Edwin Armstrong, and David Sarnoff.

MacDonald, J. Fred. *Don't Touch That Dial! Radio Programming in American Life from 1920 to 1960.* Chicago: Nelson-Hall, 1979.
> History of radio broadcasting; relates the themes of radio programs to issues in daily life.

Articles

Stock, Edwin. "Edwin Armstrong: Genius Inventor." *Audio,* November 1980, p. 53.
> Biographical article with good, brief technical explanations.

Web Sites

"First Generation Radio Archives." Available online. URL: http://www.radioarchives.org. Accessed on February 8, 2006.
> An organization dedicated to collecting, preserving, and making available recordings made from original radio broadcasts from the 1930s through the 1950s.

"The Founding Fathers of Radio." About.com. Available online. URL: http://radio.about.com/od/foundingfathers. Accessed on February 8, 2006.

Links to biographies and discussions relating to radio pioneers including Edwin Armstrong.

"Radio Pioneers & Core Technologies." Federal Communications Commission. Available online. URL: http://www.fcc.gov/omd/history/radio/Welcome.html. Accessed on February 8, 2006.

Provides an introduction and links to the ideas, inventors, and developments that made modern radio possible.

THE GHOST LIGHT

PHILO FARNSWORTH AND THE BIRTH OF TELEVISION

A 14-year-old farm boy sits atop a horse-drawn plow, driving back and forth across an Idaho potato field. The boy's mind is not on his chores. His head is full of images of electrical and electronic devices and ideas from popular science magazines. One topic in particular has captured his imagination. He has suddenly realized that electrons could be made to sweep back and forth like his father's plow, painting an image with light.

It is 1920, a time when radio broadcasting is still in its infancy. The boy, named Philo Farnsworth, is busy inventing television.

Field of Dreams

Philo Taylor Farnsworth was born on August 19, 1906, in a log cabin in rural Beaver County, Utah. His parents were descended from Mormon pioneers who had worked the land for generations—but the land was now becoming exhausted. Thus, when young Farnsworth was 11 years old, the family followed the advice of relatives and moved to a farm in Idaho's Snake River valley.

While his parents exclaimed about the fertility of the new land, Philo was more excited about the wires coming from behind the farmhouse. Unlike the old cabin, the new place was equipped with electricity, thanks to a generator. That machine was balky, though, and it kept breaking down. The family could not afford to keep paying an electrician to fix it. Philo, however, had been watching the electrician on his visits and had pestered him with numerous questions about electricity and how the generator worked. To his family's amazement, the boy offered to fix the machine, and he soon had it running again.

In addition to the generator, he found a treasure trove of popular and technical science magazines in the farmhouse attic that had been left there by the previous owners. He promptly decided to make the attic his bedroom and workshop. Soon Philo was using an assortment of parts and scrap to build an electric motor to power his mother's sewing machine. He was proud of his achievement, but his mother was less impressed. She was used to pumping the treadle of the machine, and she made him restore it to manual operation. He did have better luck when he attached motor-driven arms to the farm's washing machine. This earned the sincere gratitude of his sister Agnes, who was thus freed from hours of manual labor each week.

Most of all, Philo Farnsworth tried to get his hands on every book or article about electricity that he could find. He also stole as much time as he could from the tedious field chores that were the daily life of a farming family. Soon he was getting up at 4:00 A.M. so he would have an uninterrupted hour before the rest of the family arose. Even when he could not leave the fields, the boy could still dream of future inventions.

Fiddling with Radio

Although Philo Farnsworth's electrical talents aroused some curiosity, his father believed that it would likely be music that would be the young man's career. He had raised

Philo Farnsworth "invented" television while he was still in high school. By 1927, he had a working all-electronic TV system. (Photo courtesy of Elma G. Farnsworth)

and sold some lambs and used the money to buy a violin from a Sears catalog. He had taken lessons in the instrument at school for several years and had become so proficient that his music teacher offered him a job playing in the four-piece orchestra that provided music for the area's Friday night dances. Soon Philo could play everything from the classics to favorite sentimental tunes like "Down by the Old Mill Stream." The $5 he earned for each performance went a long way toward stocking his attic laboratory–bedroom with science textbooks and the latest technical magazines.

One of those magazines, *Science and Invention,* announced a contest for budding inventors to build a device to prevent cars from being stolen. While other contestants worked on various forms of locks or crude alarms, Philo had been studying magnetism, electricity's close cousin. One day, while plowing the field, he had another brainstorm. He obtained an ignition system from a scrapped car and magnetized it. He then magnetized a key so that only that key could turn the ignition. Farnsworth won the first prize, $25, but he did not use the money to buy science supplies. Instead, he used it to buy his first suit, so he could project a more adult appearance at the weekly dances and perhaps attract the interest of girls.

The most exciting invention in the electrical world in the early 1920s was radio. Thousands of youngsters were reading publications such as *Radio News,* edited by Hugo Gernsback, who was also busy inventing the science-fiction magazine. Articles and kits offered the opportunity to build simple radios that used crystals to tune into a small but growing number of broadcast stations. Radio in turn offered an entry into the mysterious but exciting world of electronics.

A False Start: Mechanical Television

The electrical inventions of the 19th century had focused on generating and controlling raw currents of electricity. At the turn of the new century, however, physicists had discovered the electron, the tiny particle whose behavior determined all electrical properties. Philo Farnsworth eagerly read about these new discoveries. In particular, while his high school science class was still struggling with Newton's laws, he was reading about an amazing discovery by a Swiss patent officer turned scientist—Albert Einstein. Besides revamping Newton with his theory of relativity, Einstein had also explained how electrons and light were related to each other and how a beam of light could be turned into a beam of electrons. This "photoelectric effect" particularly intrigued the boy.

With these ideas in mind, in 1922, Philo, now in high school, read an article titled "Pictures That Could Fly through the Air." While the writer provided little useful information about how this could be done, the very idea spurred Farnsworth's imagination. He began to read other articles about what was starting to be called "radio vision" or "television."

The idea of television was not actually all that new. Shortly after the telephone was introduced in 1876, cartoonists drew fanciful pictures of people watching sports events on a screen connected to a "picture telephone."

In 1884, an engineer named Paul Nipkow suggested a way to convert a picture into electrical signals. His invention consisted of a disk that had a spiral-shaped pattern of holes. As it whirled, each hole scanned across a horizontal strip of the picture. For each part of the picture, a light-sensitive bit of the rare-earth element selenium produced an electrical current in proportion to the amount of light falling on it. This information was sent along a telephone line to the receiver, which consisted of a similar wheel, electrically driven to synchronize with the transmitter. In theory, the light shining through it would reproduce the original picture.

Charles Jenkins, an American inventor, built a very crude version of this system and used it to broadcast a picture of a windmill in 1925. In 1927, President Herbert Hoover became the first politician to have his picture broadcast over the air. Jenkins called his invention "radio vision" and, as quoted by Michael Ritchie in *Please Stand By: A Prehistory of Television*, predicted that

In due course folks in California and Maine, and all the way in between, will be able to see the inauguration ceremonies of their President, in Washington; the Army and Navy football games at

Franklin Field, Philadelphia; and the struggle for supremacy in our national sport, baseball. . . . The new machine will come to the fireside as a fascinating teacher and entertainer . . . with photoplays, the opera, and a direct vision of world activities.

Jenkins was right about the impact of what would be known as television, but not about the technological road that would arrive at the televised future.

Similarly, in 1926, British inventor John Logie Baird also built a television system based on Nipkow's idea. Some sets were sold, and the British Broadcasting Company (BBC) began to broadcast TV pictures. None of these mechanical televisions worked very well, because they were slow and could not show pictures quickly enough to fool the human eye. Further, the pictures themselves were crude because they were formed from only 50 or so separate lines.

An Electronic Solution

It is at this point that Philo Farnsworth, plowing slowly across that potato field in Idaho, visualized a stream of electrons sweeping across the screen, faithfully reproducing the transmitted picture. As Paul Schatzkin, author of "The Farnsworth Chronicles," notes:

When Philo determined to learn everything he could about the subject [of television], he stepped into a Jules-Vernian world where scientists were trying to convert light into electricity with the aid of whirling discs and mirrors. Farnsworth realized right away that those discs and mirrors would never whirl fast enough to transmit a coherent image, and searched for a device that could travel at the speed of light itself. He found the solution in his invisible new friend, the electron.

Thus, one day in January 1922, as reported in "The Farnsworth Chronicles," Farnsworth's chemistry teacher, Justin Tolman, was startled to find the young man sketching electronic diagrams and equations all over the blackboard. "What has this to do with chemistry?" Tolman asked. "I've got this idea," Philo told him. "I've got to tell you about it because you're the only person I know who can understand it. This is my idea for electronic television."

Tolman had never heard the word *television* before, but the boy was persuasive. After weeks of discussions, they agreed the idea was practical. The high school student had visualized the basic idea of electronic television: a magnetically controlled beam of electrons creating an image line by line with no mechanical parts.

A Working Model

Farnsworth's plans to attend college were sidetracked when his father died and the family needed his help. Farnsworth served a brief stint in the navy. A bit later, when a temporary job as a charity fund-raiser in Salt Lake City ended, his employer, George Everson, asked him whether he was going back to school. Farnsworth replied that he could not afford school, and besides, he needed money to finance his new invention—television. He explained the idea to Everson and said that he had roughed out the basics in the lab.

Everson was intrigued with the business potential of television. When he asked Farnsworth if anyone else was working on the idea, Farnsworth explained that all the other systems were mechanical and could not be made to work properly. Finally, Everson asked Farnsworth how much money he would need to develop a working model of the system. Farnsworth suggested $5,000, though he really had no idea whether that would be enough.

As reported in "The Farnsworth Chronicles," Everson agreed and even upped the ante a bit:

> Your guess is as good as any. I surely have no idea what is involved. But I have about $6,000 in a special account in San Francisco. I've been saving it with the idea that I'd take a long shot on something and maybe make a killing. This is about as wild a gamble as I can

---

I WAS THERE: NOT WHAT IT APPEARED TO BE

In "The Farnsworth Chronicles," Paul Schatzkin recounts an incident that happened shortly after Philo Farnsworth had started assembling magnetic coils for his experimental television set:

> *Given that all this occurred in the middle of prohibition [of alcohol], it must have seemed a bit suspicious, all this unusual activity. Now, here was this total stranger in the neighborhood, sitting out in the backyard, winding copper wire around a cardboard tube. Certainly someone noticed, for one day in August, Pem [Farnsworth's wife] opened the door to find her porch filled with a small squad of blue LAPD [Los Angeles Police] uniforms, demanding to search the house. They had received a report that a still was being operated on the premises. The squad proceeded to ransack the apartment despite protests from the Farnsworths. Nothing alcoholic was found, but the sergeant was amazed by the things he did find, and began to wonder if he had stumbled on something even more sinister than a still.*
>
> *With carefully guarded words, he asked Phil what all the stuff was. Phil looked around at the strange gear he had collected, stared the sergeant straight in the eye and answered, "This is my idea for electronic television."*

---

imagine. I'll put the $6,000 up to work this thing out. If we win, it will be fine, but if we lose, I won't squawk.

At the time, Farnsworth was living in Provo, Utah. He would need to move to Los Angeles, where he would be able to draw on the resources of the superb library of the California Institute of Technology. First, however, Farnsworth proposed to his girlfriend, Emma (Pem) Gardner, that they be married in three days. Although they had grown quite fond of each other, it is still remarkable that Pem agreed to the proposal, particularly when (according to "The Farnsworth Chronicles") Farnsworth warned her on the very steps of the altar that "There is another woman in my life . . . and her name is Television!"

Demonstrations

And so, at a time when Bell Labs, Marconi Corporation, RCA, and other technological powerhouses had seemingly ended the age of the lone inventor, television was being born in an improvised laboratory.

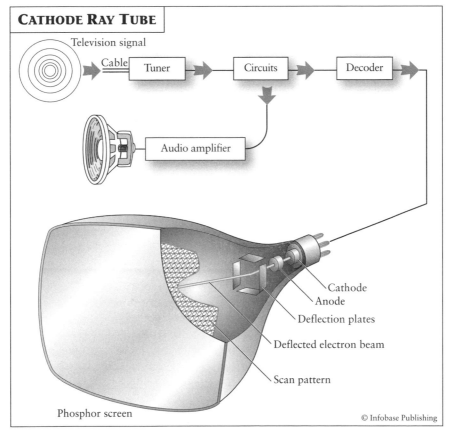

The cathode-ray tube is the heart of traditional television. The incoming signal from the tuner is fed to a decoder that converts it to instructions for controlling the flow of electrons, which are directed by magnets onto the correct spots on the screen, where phosphors serve as the pixels for the picture. (In some modern TVs, the cathode-ray tube has been replaced by light-emitting diodes (LEDs) or tiny, glowing gas lights [plasma]).

The work would be intense and prone to setbacks. This was a time when vacuum tubes were just coming into use in radio, and they were still rather unreliable. Further, the large cathode-ray tubes (CRTs), the heart of the television system, existed only in a few physics laboratories. Farnsworth's friend and partner, Cliff Gardner, had to work closely with glass blowers (and learn the art himself) in order to create the delicate tubes. Gradually, the two main components of the system took shape. The camera tube, called the image dissector, scanned the image line by line, converting the light into an electronic signal. This was then broadcast, much as with an ordinary radio signal. The receiver picked up the signal, amplified it, and converted it to the electromagnetic fields that controlled the stream of electrons that recreated the picture on the inner surface of the cathode-ray tube. Finally, on September 7, 1927, Farnsworth was able to send the image of his wife, Pem, to a receiver in an adjoining room filled with colleagues, investors, and friends.

Unfortunately, it soon became clear that much more money would be needed to design a whole new technology from the ground up. In 1928, Farnsworth got an appointment to see W. W. Crocker, a famous San Francisco banker. By then, the television system was far enough along that it could transmit a simple fixed image reliably. When one of Crocker's bankers asked "When are we going to see some dollars in this thing?" Farnsworth responded by throwing a switch. The image of a dollar sign glowed on the screen. Crocker agreed to invest $25,000 on the condition that Farnsworth move his lab to San Francisco.

One day in 1928, Farnsworth was looking at the television screen and saw wisps of smoke in the picture. He was afraid the lab was on fire (always a danger with the delicate tubes)—but then he saw a hand with a cigarette waving in the picture. Cliff Gardner had been smoking while working on the TV camera. The clarity of the smoke swirls in the picture told Farnsworth that they had been making considerable progress in sharpening the picture. Soon they continued their tests with moving pictures, gradually gaining the ability to project a movie on a screen, scan it through the television camera, and broadcast it to the receiver.

By the end of 1928, the system was essentially complete, and the patents had been filed. Farnsworth and his backers now needed the money and business connections to begin manufacturing and marketing it.

Skirmishes and Detours

Meanwhile, David Sarnoff and the giant Radio Corporation of America (RCA) had begun to enter the field of television. Sarnoff, a visionary who had predicted the impact of commercial radio broadcasting in 1915, had decided that television would be the technology that would keep RCA profitable and ahead of the competition.

Sarnoff hired a Russian inventor named Vladimir Zworykin to develop an RCA television system. Sarnoff had heard about Farnsworth's work, and he asked Zworykin to visit Farnsworth but not to tell him about RCA's interest in television. After receiving Zworykin's report suggesting that Farnsworth's system was just about ready to be marketed, Sarnoff was alarmed. It would not only take RCA some time to come up with its own television system, it was also doubtful whether they could do it without Farnsworth granting permission to use his patents. Sarnoff offered Farnsworth $100,000 for his entire operation, plus a job as an engineer with RCA.

Sarnoff could probably have simply paid Farnsworth for the right to use his patents—a common arrangement in many industries. Legend had it, though, that Sarnoff always insisted that "The Radio Corporation does not pay patent royalties, we collect them." RCA and the American Telegraph and Telephone Company (AT&T), for example, had made an arrangement so that each could use the other's patents as long as AT&T stayed out of broadcasting and RCA didn't try to compete in the telephone market. "Patent monopolies" like this made it very difficult for upstarts like Farnsworth to enter the market, and they eventually aroused the attention of federal regulators.

Farnsworth and his backers had already spent considerably more than $100,000 on the project, and they considered Sarnoff's proposal to be an insult, not a serious offer. Farnsworth then found what seemed to be a suitable business partner in the Philco Corporation (no relation to Philo), a radio company that had managed to compete successfully with RCA. With the aid of Philco's resources, they began to fine-tune their TV system. Paul Schatzkin notes that

> *[Farnsworth] set up a prototype receiver in his home, and [his son] little Philo III became the first charter member of the "television generation." His usual program diet consisted of a Mickey Mouse cartoon, "Steamboat Willy," which ran over and over again through the film chain at the laboratory several miles away. While little Philo watched, his father and the engineers at Philco made adjustments and tuned the circuits.*

As research continued, Farnsworth improved his television system in a number of ways. He added an "electron multiplier" to create a brighter image in the tube. An improved magnetic deflector allowed the system to form a brighter picture containing 220 lines.

Farnsworth's working relationship with Philco began to break down, however. Philco executives were demanding more control over the development of the television system, and they also seemed to be working with Farnsworth's partners behind his back. He started a new company, Farnsworth Television.

In 1934, Farnsworth put on the first public demonstration of electronic television at the Franklin Institute in Philadelphia. He broadcast a variety of programs from an improvised studio on the roof of the building. Thousands of visitors took 15-minute turns to see vaudeville acts and short speeches by assorted politicians on the small, round screen.

Battle of the Patents

Meanwhile, RCA had launched a full-scale legal attack on Farnsworth's television patents. They tried to claim that Zworykin's unpatented television ideas of 1923 should take precedence over Farnsworth's 1927 system. When Farnsworth claimed that he had come up with the essential ideas of television while he was still in high school, the RCA attorneys laughed. Farnsworth's lawyer then put chemistry teacher Justin Tolman on the stand. Tolman recalled his detailed conversation with the young Farnsworth, and amazingly, sketched an electronic television tube from memory—a tube identical in essential features to the disputed invention!

In April 1934, the U.S. Patent Office found in favor of Farnsworth on all counts. The decision could be appealed in court, however, and that's what RCA did, relying on their "deep pockets" and believing that Farnsworth would go broke because no one would invest in a system that was tied up in litigation.

I WAS THERE: UNSUNG HERO

In 1957, Philo Farnsworth finally appeared on the millions of televisions that had sprung from his original vision. It was a popular show called *I've Got a Secret,* where a group of panelists tried to guess the identity of the "mystery guest." Farnsworth was identified as "Dr. X" and outside the panelists' view, the audience was told that Farnsworth's secret was "I invented electronic television."

The panelists naturally assumed that "Dr. X" was some sort of medical doctor. One asked if he had invented some kind of machine that might be painful when used. Farnsworth slyly agreed: "Yes, sometimes, it's most painful." None of them could guess who Farnsworth was, so he won the $80 prize.

Even as late as the 1990s, Farnsworth's role as inventor of television remained largely unknown to the public who used his invention for so many hours every day. When Paul Schatzkin, author of "The Farnsworth Chronicles," tried to interest CBS in creating a documentary about the inventor, a network official replied as follows:

> *Although television itself is of paramount interest to all of us, it is my feeling that this alone does not make the life of the man who invented television necessarily of dramatic interest. His trials and tribulations on the way to fame and fortune are familiar to the American success story and so too his ultimate rejection of the fruits of his own invention. . . . It is rare when a true life story has the appropriate ingredients so that it plays out less as biography and more like a movie.*

While the legal case played out in the courts, Farnsworth went to Great Britain and received $50,000 from Baird Television—John Logie Baird had finally realized that their mechanical television system was no longer adequate. A later trip to Germany was less successful—by the mid-1930s, the Nazis were in power, and they essentially stole the Farnsworth patent and refused to pay royalties. Their broadcast of the 1936 Olympic Games in Berlin would mark the first use of television as a tool of propaganda.

After Farnsworth returned from abroad, he and his partners quarreled. The partners wanted to see a financial return sooner rather than later, but Farnsworth wanted to be an inventor who developed and licensed patents, not a manufacturer.

When the courts finally upheld Farnsworth's patent, RCA did pay Farnsworth to use it. Sarnoff's genius for publicity turned the New York World's Fair of 1939 into a showcase for television as an RCA product. RCA set up an impressive display and even built the first mobile TV news van to broadcast events live from the scene.

Fading Away

As the 1930s wore on, Farnsworth's struggle to bring his television system to fruition took an increasing toll on his personal life. Farnsworth's relationship with his wife, Pem, had already suffered a serious blow in 1932 when their 18-month-old son, Kenny, died of a throat infection. Philco executives refused to allow Farnsworth to take time off to attend his son's burial in Provo, Utah. Pem felt abandoned and betrayed, a victim of Farnsworth's "other woman," television. Farnsworth also became depressed, seeking relief in periodic bouts of drinking that gradually turned into alcoholism.

When the United States entered World War II at the end of 1941, the development of commercial television was put on hold. Farnsworth, who had suffered a severe nervous breakdown in 1940, would spend the war on the sidelines.

Following the war, the television market exploded. The 8,000 television sets in the United States in 1946 became a million by 1949 and 10 million only two years later. By then, however, Farnsworth's main television patent had expired. Farnsworth's company had a brief burst

The first televised American presidential debate. John F. Kennedy may have beaten Richard Nixon because he looked better on TV. (Smithsonian Institution Photo no. 84-10773)

of activity, but it was too late. Mounting debts had brought the company to the brink of bankruptcy, and it was sold to the International Telephone and Telegraph Corporation (IT&T) in the spring of 1949.

By 1960, television had become a ubiquitous presence in the home. In the coming decade, television became a vital part of political campaigns as well as the preferred source of news about tragedies of war and assassinations, as well as about triumphs such as the Apollo Moon landings.

The Transfiguration of TV

In succeeding decades, television changed in several ways. The most visible was the addition of color. Early color television systems proposed before World War II by various inventors used wheels and suffered from the same drawbacks as other mechanical systems. Practical color TV began to appear increasingly in American homes in the 1960s, led by RCA's development of a system that used three separate electron beams that activated separate sets of red, green, and blue dots on the screen. While color TV was expensive at first, by 1972 more than half of all television sets in American homes were color models.

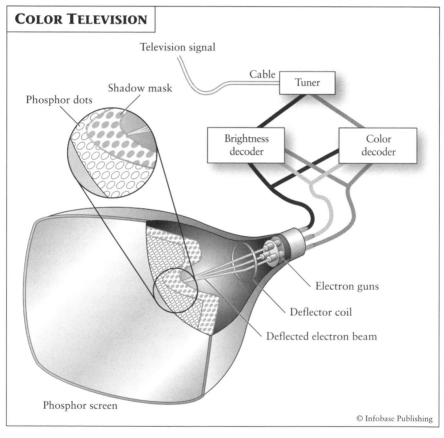

COLOR TELEVISION

Television signal

Cable

Tuner

Shadow mask

Phosphor dots

Brightness decoder

Color decoder

Electron guns

Deflector coil

Deflected electron beam

Phosphor screen

© Infobase Publishing

Color television uses two separate signals, one for brightness and one that contains three color levels (red, green, and blue). A color decoder extracts information from the color signal to control a separate electron gun for each color. The picture is colored by combining the glowing dots activated by the beams.

Perhaps more important even than color were changes in the way television programs were delivered to viewers. Until the 1980s, television in the United States was dominated by the three big networks, NBC, ABC, and CBS. The networks produced the most important programs and thus decided what would be shown. But two new technologies, cable and satellite, would greatly increase the choices available to the TV viewer.

Cable TV started back in the 1940s as a way to get programming to remote communities that could not receive broadcast signals. In the 1960s, cable companies offered the technology as a way to provide better reception, free of "snow" and "ghosts." In the later 1970s and 1980s, however, cable companies began to offer not just better pictures but more choices. Together with direct satellite broadcasting to home "dish" receivers, cable brought to viewers programs ranging from recent movies on HBO and other channels to scientific and historical documentaries to political debates live from the floor of Congress on CSPAN. The launch of the Cable News Network (CNN) soon challenged the news monopoly of the three older networks.

Where the broadcast networks had to program for the widest possible audience, cable and satellite were able to carry from tens to hundreds of separate channels, making room for just about every interest, as well as broadcasting in dozens of languages.

Many of today's television sets would have perplexed Philo Farnsworth. Instead of a bulky cathode-ray tube, the display consists of a flat panel with layers of liquid crystals (LCDs) that pass or block light according to the digital signal they receive. Huge plasma or rear projection screens in "home theaters" fill the wall of many living rooms.

At the beginning of the new century, television seems to be on the brink of an even deeper transformation in how it is delivered and viewed. Many programs are now available for download from the Internet for display on personal computers. And portability has taken on new levels: In 2005, Apple released a model of its popular iPod music player that can play video files, and viewers now have the option of buying certain current TV programs directly from the network to view when and where they wish. Meanwhile, thanks to the video cassette recorder (VCR) and its successors, DVDs and digital video recorders, even traditional television is now at the viewer's disposal at any time or place. (By 2006, the You Tube Web site was showing 100 million video clips daily.)

Television, like the telephone, has split into myriad forms and choices. It has become part of the information superhighway, a long way from the electronic dreams of a young boy in a potato field.

Belated Recognition

By the late 1950s, Farnsworth had lost interest in television, which he felt had betrayed its promise as a tool for education and a source of quality entertainment. Farnsworth became intrigued by another idea. In developing tubes where electrons were accelerated and slammed into the screen, Farnsworth had seen a mysterious blue glow. With the growing interest in nuclear power at the time, Farnsworth wondered whether such tubes could be used to produce nuclear fusion reactions. If so, it could mean an inexhaustible source of power that was far more compact and easier to handle than the bulky, relatively dangerous nuclear-fission reactors being developed. Unfortunately, like the somewhat similar "cold-fusion" experiments of the late 1980s, this idea proved to be a dead end.

Philo Farnsworth died on March 11, 1971, after a succession of increasingly debilitating illnesses. His life and achievements were little remarked at the time. (Sarnoff, who died only nine months later, was hailed as the father of television broadcasting.)

Gradually, though, Farnsworth began to receive recognition and to attract some public interest. In 1984, the U.S. Postal Service issued a set of postage stamps that honored Farnsworth among other largely forgotten inventors such as Edwin Armstrong and Nikola Tesla. This recognition in turn led the National Inventors Hall of Fame to add Farnsworth to its role of honor (Vladimir Zworykin had been inducted in 1977).

In 1989, a group of students in Farnsworth's birth state of Utah researched the inventor's life. They noted that in the National Statuary Hall in the U.S. Capitol each state was entitled to have two statutes to honor its distinguished citizens. At the time, Utah had only a statue of Brigham Young, the Mormon leader who had founded the state. The students successfully petitioned to add

Farnsworth as its second honoree. In 1990, a statue of Farnsworth was erected. He is shown holding a tube in his hand, upon a base inscribed "Father of Television."

The 1990s brought the World Wide Web, and with it, an explosion in Web sites seeking to bring little-known inventors and other historical figures to light. Sites such as Paul Schatzkin's "The Farnsworth Chronicles" have made stories of inventors such as Farnsworth accessible and exciting, even as computers and the Internet began to challenge the dominance of the television networks. By then, Farnsworth's struggle to create new forms of communication in makeshift laboratories was being echoed by computer and Web developers working in garages and low-rent offices.

Finally, on September 22, 2002, the television industry itself finally paid its respects to its inventor. The 54th annual Emmy Awards were dedicated to Farnsworth, and his widow, Pem, was present to receive a special award. In 2004 came word that a movie about Farnsworth's life was to be written by Aaron Sorkin, creator of the award-winning TV series *The West Wing*. Although the project was later cancelled, Sorkin plans to reconceive it as a stage play.

Chronology

1884	Paul Nipkow invents a crude form of mechanical television
1897	The cathode-ray tube is invented. For a long time, it will only be used for physics experiments
1906	Philo Farnsworth is born on August 19 in a log cabin in rural Utah
1918	Farnsworth's family moves to a farm in Idaho where he reads science magazines, fixes a generator, and designs a magnetic car-ignition key
1920	Farnsworth gets the idea for electronic television while plowing a potato field
1922	In January, Farnsworth sketches his idea for electronic television on the blackboard of his chemistry class

1926	Farnsworth marries Elma (Pem) Gardner on May 27 and moves to Los Angeles
1927	Charles Jenkins's "radio vision" broadcasts a speech by President Herbert Hoover. However, mechanical television proves to be a dead end
	In September, Farnsworth first demonstrates his electronic television system
1928	Farnsworth broadcasts a dollar sign to impress W. W. Crocker's bankers
	Farnsworth perfects his television system
1934	Farnsworth demonstrates his electronic television system at the Franklin Institute in Philadelphia
	The U.S. Patent Office finds in favor of Farnsworth. Farnsworth also eventually prevails in the courts
1936	Nazis broadcast the Berlin Olympics on a Farnsworth TV system, having harassed the inventor and refused to pay royalties
1939	RCA, having finally bought access to the Farnsworth patent, puts on a spectacular TV demonstration at the New York World's Fair
1941–45	World War II halts most television development
1947	Farnsworth's main television patent expires just as the industry is finally booming
1949	Farnsworth's television company goes bankrupt and is sold to IT&T
1950s	Television grows rapidly in extent and importance, but Farnsworth loses interest in the field and begins pursuing his idea about nuclear fusion
1957	Farnsworth appears on *I've Got a Secret* but no panelist recognizes him
1971	Farnsworth dies on March 11

1984	A set of U.S. postage stamps honor Farnsworth and other "forgotten" inventors
1990	A statute of Farnsworth is erected in the U.S. Capitol
1990s	Web sites help spur recognition of Farnsworth's achievements
2002	Farnsworth is honored with a special Emmy Award presented to his widow, Pem
2004	A movie script called *The Farnsworth Invention* is written by Aaron Sorkin, producer of *The West Wing*. Production is later cancelled but the work may appear as a play
2005	Apple releases the video iPod
2005	You Tube Web Site shows 100 million videos daily

Further Reading

Books

Farnsworth, Pem. *Distant Vision: Romance and Discovery on the Invisible Frontier.* Salt Lake City: Pemberly Kent Press, 1994.
    Biography of Farnsworth by his widow; brought many previously unknown details to light.
McPherson, Stephanie S. *TV's Forgotten Hero: The Story of Philo Farnsworth.* Minneapolis: Lerner Group, 1996.
    Biography of Farnsworth for young readers.
Ritchie, Michael. *Please Stand By: A Prehistory of Television.* Woodstock, N.Y.: Overlook Press, 1994.
    A history of early television broadcasting, focusing more on the programs than on the technical developments.
Schatzkin, Paul. *The Boy Who Invented Television.* Silver Spring, Md.: TeamCom Books, 2002.
    Biography of Farnsworth by the creator of the Farnsworth Chronicles Web site.
Schwartz, Evan I. *The Last Lone Inventor: David Sarnoff vs. Philo T. Farnsworth.* New York: HarperCollins, 2002.
    A dual biography that focuses on how Farnsworth's and Sarnoff's ambitions brought them into conflict with each other.

Articles

Schwartz, Evan I. "Who Really Invented Television?" *Technology Review* 103 (September 2000): 96.

> Describes how Farnsworth finally won a legal victory, at great personal cost. Compares the dominance of David Sarnoff and RCA to the modern position of Bill Gates and Microsoft.

Web Sites

David Sarnoff Library. URL: http://www.davidsarnoff.org. Accessed on November 10, 2005.

> This site is dedicated to the life and career of David Sarnoff, and features the extensive resources of the Sarnoff museum and library. Includes a biography and time line.

"The Farnsworth Chronicles." By Paul Schatzkin. URL: http://www.farnovision.com/chronicles. Accessed on November 10, 2005.

> Farnsworth's story and related matters, told in an engaging style in this resource-rich site. The site has played an important role in publicizing Farnsworth's key role in television history.

7

UNLOCKING THE SIGNALS

CLAUDE SHANNON, COMMUNICATIONS, AND INFORMATION THEORY

By the middle of the 20th century, the vast telephone network had become an integral part of daily life in all industrialized nations, connecting millions of subscribers. The maturing radio and television industries were also contributing to the complexity of electronic transmission networks. New electronic-switching devices were being used to increase the capacity and reach of the network. There was a growing problem, however. The exploding complexity of the network was threatening to make it unmanageable just as war and the postwar industrial boom made communications increasingly necessary.

The root of this growing problem was not just technological. Despite growing understanding of electronic hardware, little was known about how that vital but intangible thing called "information" fared when it traveled through the wires or air. A mathematician-engineer named Claude Shannon would provide a vitally needed theory, creating a new discipline of information science at the dawn of the computer age.

Claude Shannon was born in Gaylord, Michigan, on April 30, 1916. His family was respectably professional: Shannon's father was an attorney and probate judge, while his mother was a language teacher and high school principal. One of Shannon's

Claude Shannon developed the mathematical information theory that enabled engineers to create and control the vast communications networks of the second half of the 20th century. (Reprinted with permission of Lucent Technologies Inc./Bell Labs)

grandfathers had patented several inventions, while one of his more distant cousins was an even more famous inventor—Thomas Edison.

Shannon was one of those youngsters who love to tinker with anything mechanical or electrical. He took radios apart and even built a working telegraph system linking his house to that of a friend about half a mile away. After talking the local phone company into giving him some surplus equipment, Shannon later "upgraded" the service from telegraph to telephone.

When Shannon enrolled in the University of Michigan in 1932, he first set his sights on a degree and career in electrical engineering. However, as he was exposed to advanced mathematics courses, he became intrigued by math and symbolic logic. He especially became interested in the relationship of logical symbols and operations to real-world circuits and switching systems. In 1936, Shannon graduated with bachelor's degrees in both mathematics and electrical engineering.

Logical Circuits

One day, as a graduate student, Shannon saw a notice on a bulletin board, looking for someone to run a machine called a differential analyzer. This complicated analog computer had been built by Vannevar Bush at the Massachusetts Institute of Technology. Unlike a modern digital computer, an analog computer uses physical properties (such as electrical characteristics) to perform calculations or simulations. Before a "program" could be run on the machine, a complicated circuit had to be created and data input manually in the form of voltage levels and other physical quantities.

Working with all these details, Shannon realized that "Boolean logic" (comparison operations such as AND, OR, and NOT) could be used to represent the states of the various switches within the machine and the operations to be carried out. In 1938, Shannon wrote a master's thesis titled "A Symbolic Analysis of Relay and Switching Circuits." This paper so impressed the engineering world that it was given the Alfred Nobel prize (not to be confused with the more famous Nobel Prize given in Sweden). As Shannon later told an interviewer for *Omni* magazine, "That was a lot of fun, working that out. I had more fun doing that than anything else in my life."

A Theory of Communication

In 1941, Shannon joined Bell Laboratories. The spiritual descendant of Edison's "invention factory," Bell Labs had become the nation's leading industrial research organization. Unlike labs that focused on

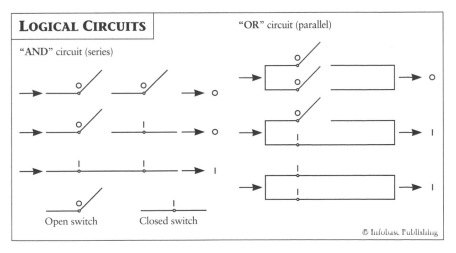

In his early work, Shannon showed that any logical operation could be modeled using simple circuits such as series (AND) or parallel (OR). Here, the binary 1 represents a closed switch, and a 0 represents an open one.

developing specific products or pursuing short-term research, Bell Labs scientists were free to look at fundamental topics. Now, on the eve of World War II, Bell, the world's largest phone company, asked its researchers for help in expanding a telephone system that would soon require millions of new lines. Further, the government was also seeking help with cryptography—how to secure one's own transmissions while finding ways to break opponents' codes. Since Shannon was already avidly pursuing an interest in information transmission and cryptography, he was a perfect fit as a new researcher at the lab.

Shannon's research on cryptography resulted in a paper titled "A Mathematical Theory of Cryptography," but for security reasons, it would not be published until after the war. A much larger and more immediate impact came from another Shannon paper, "A Mathematical Theory of Communication," published in 1948 in the *Bell System Technical Journal.*

Practical engineers and even many theorists tended to consider each form of transmission to be a different problem: A telephone call passing through a wire dealt with one kind of circuit, while radio transmissions used very different forms of energy and electronic devices. Further, the common terminology of electrical or electronic engineers dealt with such things as wavelengths and signal strengths and the effect of different circuits, components, or natural phenomena on the signal. Little attention was paid to the actual contents of a signal.

Starting in 1939, however, as Shannon noted in a letter to Vannevar Bush, he had "been working on an analysis of some of the fundamental properties of general systems for the transmission of intelligence [information], including telephony radio, television, telegraphy, etc."

The Information Equation

Shannon stepped back from those details and began with a new fundamental perspective, one that information theorist Robert Gallager (as quoted by M. Mitchell Waldrop) believed would result in "a blueprint for the digital age" of the next half century. Shannon looked to *information* as the key to communication and asked, "What determines the extent to which the information intended by the sender can be received and recovered by the receiver?"

In his paper, Shannon identified the fundamental unit of information as the binary digit, or "bit," which would become familiar to computer users. One bit, after all, could be a yes-or-no answer to a previously agreed-upon question. More complex transmissions, of course, require many bits to stand for characters, numbers, or perhaps pixels in a picture.

Shannon pointed out that in any communications system there is:

- A device that encodes the information in some suitable form, such as interruptions in current (telegraph) or variations (telephone)
- A channel or medium through which the message is sent (such as a wire or in the case of radio, the atmosphere)
- A receiving device that detects and extracts the coded information from the signal
- One or more sources of "noise" (interference or distortion) that threaten to obliterate or garble the bits of information

Along with the prolific mathematician John von Neumann, Shannon had begun to see a connection between the flow of information and that of energy in the physical universe. In physics, the concept of entropy refers to "usable" energy, energy that is available to do work. If, for example, hot (energetic) air molecules are together in the form of steam, they can turn a turbine to create power. Eventually, molecules become randomized, reaching an equilibrium temperature where no more work can be done—the state of maximum entropy. In the course of things, any closed system (to which no new energy is being added) always moves toward maximum entropy.

Similarly, Shannon showed that any data transmission involves a struggle between the ordered patterns that can carry information and the randomization caused by various sources of noise. Noise randomizes the text, perhaps changing "What hath God wrought" to "Whst oath God wxlughr." At some point, the randomization renders the message unintelligible. (Another key concept is the connection between information and *uncertainty*. Something is only information if it tells the receiver something he or she does not already know.)

Shannon showed how to measure the redundancy, or duplication, within a stream of data, relating it to the transmitting channel's capacity, or bandwidth. Redundancy offsets the garbling effects of noise. For example, if the message "What hath God wrought" is repeated three times in the message, they can be compared letter for letter. If two of the messages have "What" and one has "Whst," the latter can be disregarded. The cost of redundancy is that fewer distinct messages can be transmitted in a channel with a given capacity.

It turned out to be a matter of probabilities of error—probabilities that could be controlled. For any channel, if the bandwidth is large enough in comparison to the message, an error-free transmission can be assured. (For some applications, such as sending pictures, a small amount of error is acceptable, in exchange for requiring less data be sent per picture.)

Finally, Shannon went on to devise methods that could be used to automatically find and correct errors in the transmission.

Transforming Communications

In the depth and scope of his achievements, Shannon essentially founded modern information theory, which would become vital for technology as diverse as computer networks, broadcasting, data compression, and data storage on media such as disks, CDs, and DVDs.

Looking back from the vantage point of 2001, artificial-intelligence researcher Marvin Minsky told NPR interviewer Robert Siegel that Shannon's paper "had almost everything that was discovered afterwards with thousands of people in psychology and mathematics and physics working on it."

For the practical engineers, Shannon's theory meant that that the way was clear to improve existing communications and digital storage technologies and to develop new ones, increasing the bandwidth while maintaining the needed accuracy. Thus, Robert Lucky, a research executive at one of today's offshoots of Bell Labs, noted to M. Mitchell Waldrop that

For 50 years, people have worked to get to the channel capacity [Shannon] said was possible. Only recently have we gotten close. His influence was profound.

Shannon was disturbed however, when by the 1950s his information theory was being touted as an all-purpose way of explaining

---

CONNECTIONS: BUILDING A MULTIMEDIA WORLD

Although most consumers are unaware of the details of information theory, every day they use its principles in the form of electronic products and services that enrich their lives with information, education, and of course, entertainment. The cable and satellite TV systems that feed video signals into millions of American homes use video-encoding techniques that date back to Shannon's original work and to that of other Bell Labs researchers, allowing maximum use of bandwidth while minimizing transmission errors.

Similarly, modern data-encoding compression techniques based on information theory allow millions of young (and not so young) people to fill their iPods and MP3 players with the equivalent of a shelf full of CDs. Photo formats such as JPEG maximize the number of pictures that can be taken with a digital camera before changing memory cards. Photographers can choose between "lossless" (completely accurate) images that take more disk space and various degrees of compression that make the images much more compact at some cost in accuracy.

Other devices that depend on efficient data storage are also reshaping the world of broadcasting. Personal digital video recorders are changing how and when people watch television programs, as is the ability to "stream" programs on demand over the Internet and play them on a wide variety of devices.

Without the ability to understand how to design transmission formats to use the bandwidth of channels such as network cable, fiber optics, telephone, and wireless (WiFi), this world of ever-richer digital media would not have been possible. That is the legacy Claude Shannon has given to both engineers and consumers.

just about everything in the universe. "Information," after all, is a slippery concept. Do the radio emissions of stars like the Sun truly contain information in the sense that an Earthly radio broadcast does? For Shannon, information had to be something that "meant something" to the receiver. Shannon tried to use language precisely, but popular concepts have a life of their own.

Artificial-Intelligence Pioneer

Bell Labs did not limit its researchers to topics that were directly related to telephone systems or even communications and information theory in general. In 1943, Bell Labs was visited by Alan Turing, the British mathematician who had done for computing theory what Shannon was beginning to do for communications theory. The two researchers began to share ideas during afternoon breaks. Shannon became one of a handful of researchers who saw a unique potential in the electronic digital computers that had been developed during the war. In particular, Shannon wanted to see whether computers could perform tasks that most people would assume would require intelligence. In other words, he had begun to pursue the question of artificial intelligence (AI). In 1950, Shannon published an article in *Scientific American* that gave algorithms, or procedures that could enable a computer to play chess.

While Shannon's work dealt in abstraction and mathematical theory, it was never divorced from physical reality. In his NPR interview, Marvin Minsky explained that

> [Shannon] had ideas about artificial intelligence. . . . I became a protégé [disciple] of his. And I was really inspired by the fact that whenever there was a problem, he would say, "Well, let's solve it. Let's do something." And that amazing thing was that ... if he did prove a theorem mathematically, that wasn't enough. He would get out a hammer and saw or a milling machine and he would build some gadget that would show that it actually works. He was very good at machinery.

The first electronic digital computers (such as the ENIAC shown here) arrived in the mid-1940s. They offered both challenges and opportunities for applying information and communications theory. (U.S. Army Photo)

Shannon also became interested in "teaching" machines to navigate in the physical world. He built an electronic "mouse" that could solve mazes with the aid of simple but interesting logic circuits. As the 1950s progressed, researchers began to formally organize the field of artificial intelligence. Along with such pioneers as John McCarthy and Marvin Minsky, Shannon was a contributor to a collection of papers titled *Automata Studies*.

Teacher and Writer

Toward the end of the decade, Shannon's focus shifted from research to teaching. As Donner Professor of Science at MIT (1958–78) Shannon

I WAS THERE: SHANNON'S HOUSE OF GADGETS

Even after his retirement, Shannon intrigued visitors at his home. As writer John Horgan of *Scientific American* recounted in 1990:

Without waiting for an answer, and over the mild protests of his wife, Betty, [Shannon] leaps from his chair and disappears into the other room. When I catch up with him, he proudly shows me his seven chess-playing machines, gasoline-powered pogo stick, hundred-bladed jackknife, two-seated unicycle and countless other marvels.

Some of Shannon's gadgets expressed his lifelong interest in balancing and juggling. He was an accomplished builder of unicycles, including one that was deliberately designed with its single wheel "off center" so he could juggle balls while riding. Shannon also built elaborate mechanical juggling machines, including a complete miniature "circus" consisting of three clowns juggling 11 rings, seven balls, and five clubs, all under the control of elaborate clockwork.

Shannon's chess-playing machines moved the pieces with mechanical arms while occasionally issuing wry remarks. An even less practical invention was "THROBAC," a calculator that did its mathematical operations using Roman numerals. Shannon's most wryly amusing device, however, was the "Universal Machine." One of Shannon's visitors, the science-fiction writer Arthur C. Clarke, describes the device in his *Voices across the Sea:*

Nothing could be simpler. It is merely a small wooden casket, the size and shape of a cigar box, with a single switch on one face. When you throw the switch, there is an angry, purposeful buzzing. The lid slowly rises, and from beneath it emerges a hand. The hand reaches down, turns the switch off, and retreats into the box. With the finality of a closing coffin, the lid snaps shut, the buzzing ceases and peace reigns once more.

lectured on artificial-intelligence topics. He also explored the social impacts of automation and computer technology as a Fellow at the Center for the Study of Behavioral Sciences in Palo Alto, California.

MIT information scientist Robert Fano is quoted by M. Mitchell Waldrop as recalling about Shannon: "He wrote beautiful papers—when he wrote. And he gave beautiful talks—when he gave a talk. But he hated to do it." Waldrop suggested that Shannon was in some ways a shy person; he shunned fame and publicity. It was enough for him to know that he knew the answer to a question that intrigued him.

It was only during the last decade of his life that Shannon was gradually overtaken by Alzheimer's disease, which had (ironically, perhaps) gradually degraded the signals coming from his remarkable mind. Shannon died on February 26, 2001, in Murray Hill, New Jersey. Shannon had been honored with numerous awards, including the Institute of Electrical and Electronics Engineers (IEEE) Medal of Honor and the National Medal of Technology (both awarded in 1996). Shannon was also elected (with Bernard Oliver) to the National Inventors Hall of Fame for their invention of a high-speed digital transmission system based on coded electronic pulses.

Although the Nobel Prize is not awarded for mathematics, Marvin Minsky said in his NPR interview that Shannon's stature was comparable to that of Albert Einstein's as someone whose life and work could answer the question, "Who's a scientist?"

Chronology

1916	Claude Shannon is born on April 30 in Gaylord, Michigan
1936	Shannon graduates from the University of Michigan with degrees in mathematics and electrical engineering
	Shannon goes to MIT and works with Vannevar Bush and his differential analyzer
1937	Shannon publishes his paper "A Symbolic Analysis of Relay and Switching Circuits"
1941	Shannon joins Bell Labs
1943	Shannon meets Alan Turing and begins to discuss information theory with him and John Neumann. He also writes a classified paper on cryptographic theory

1948	Shannon's paper "A Mathematical Theory of Communication" essentially creates modern information theory
1950	Shannon publishes an article on how to design a chess-playing computer program
1950s	Shannon, together with researchers such as Marvin Minsky and John McCarthy, helps establish the field of artificial intelligence
1958	Shannon becomes a professor at MIT and shifts from research to teaching
1978	Shannon retires
1996	Shannon receives the National Medal of Technology
2001	Shannon dies on February 26 after a long struggle with Alzheimer's disease

Further Reading

Books

Shannon, Claude. *Collected Papers*. New York: Wiley-IEEE Press, 1993.

> Contains Shannon's complete scientific works, including some not previously published. In addition to communications, switching theory, and cryptography, there are also papers on population genetics and even the theory of juggling.

Articles

Horgan, John. "Claude E. Shannon: Unicyclist, Juggler and Father of Information Theory." *Scientific American,* January 1990, p. 22ff.

> A fascinating account of Shannon's wide-ranging interests and inventions.

"Information Theory." Lucent Technologies/Bell Labs. Available online. URL: http://www.lucent.com/minds/infotheory. Accessed on August 28, 2006.

> A useful introduction to information theory and the work of Claude Shannon; includes link to a more detailed overview.

"Interview: Claude Shannon." *Omni,* August 1987, pp. 61–66, 110. (Also included in Shannon's *Collected Papers*).
>Includes interesting reflections by Shannon on his life and work.

Shannon, Claude. "A Chess-Playing Machine." *Scientific American,* February 1950, pp. 48–51.
>The first popular account explaining how a machine could play chess.

———. "A Mathematical Theory of Communication." *Bell System Technical Journal* 27 (July–October 1948): 379–423, 623–656. Also available online. URL: http://cm.bell-labs.com/cm/ms/what/ shannonday/shannon1948.pdf. Accessed on February 1, 2006.
>Shannon's groundbreaking paper on communications theory; gives clear conceptual explanations that are useful even for readers who lack sufficient mathematical background to follow all the details.

Siegel, Robert. "Marvin Minsky Talks about the Late Dr. Claude Shannon." National Public Radio. Available online. URL: http://www.npr.org/templates/story/story.php?storyId=1119186. Accessed on February 1, 2006.
>Audio file of interview in 2001 on NPR's "All Things Considered," in which Marvin Minsky praises his late colleague's groundbreaking work in fundamental communications theory and artificial intelligence.

Waldrop, M. Mitchell. "Claude Shannon: Reluctant Father of the Digital Age." *Technology Review,* July/August 2001, pp. 64–71.
>Describes the significance of Shannon's work on communications theory and how it relates to technologies taken for granted today.

8

COMMUNICATING WITH COMPUTERS

JOSEPH LICKLIDER AND THE INTERNET

The development of electrical communication in the 19th century and electronic broadcasting in the first half of the 20th century was largely the work first of informally trained inventors and later of members of the new profession of electrical engineering. They were joined by mathematicians and physicists who could provide a deeper understanding of the interactions of moving electrons and electromagnetic waves.

By the middle of the 20th century, however, pioneers in computer and communications theory (such as Claude Shannon) were highlighting the importance of information processing. By leaving the realm of electronic circuits and considering how people perceive and understand information, other disciplines such as neurology and psychology come into play. It becomes necessary to take a larger view of communications that sees the people using the system as an integral part of the overall network.

John Carl Robnett Licklider would do much to bring this new perspective to communications theory. Trained in psychology as well as electronics and computing, Licklider would focus on how people could use the new technology of the post–World War II era to communicate and access information. In doing so, he would inspire and guide much of the effort to build a new kind of communications network: the Internet.

Models, Machines, and Minds

Licklider was born on March 11, 1915, in St. Louis, Missouri. His father was a self-made man who had started as a farmer but then worked on the railroad to support his family when his own father died. Later, he became an advertising writer and a successful insurance agent.

Young Licklider, called Rob (and later, Lick) by his friends, shared the passion for flight that had been ignited in so many people by the exploits of Charles Lindbergh and other pioneer aviators of the 1920s. Rob learned to carve intricate model airplanes from wood. At the age of 16, though, he took up another interest of young men—cars. His parents bought him an old "clunker" on the condition that he would not actually drive it off their

Joseph Licklider's background in psychology and engineering would enable him to create new ways for users to interact and communicate with computers. (AIP Emilio Segrè Visual Archives, Gallery of Member Society Presidents)

property. The intrepid teenager took the car completely apart and painstakingly put it back together until he understood how every part worked.

During the 1930s, Licklider attended Washington University in St. Louis, pursuing a variety of interests. By the time he was done, Licklider had earned not only one B.A. degree but three— in psychology, mathematics, and physics. He then decided to focus on psychology, earning an M.A. at Washington University in 1938 and then a Ph.D. from the University of Rochester in 1942. This combination of psychological training and grounding in the tools of the physical sciences would well equip Licklider to work with the complicated interface between machines and their users.

The New Brain Science

To most people in the 1940s, "psychology" meant one of two things. One was the "academic psychology" that sought to understand behavior through experiment, but had little detailed knowledge of how the brain actually worked. The other was the abstract or symbolic systems of Freud and the other psychoanalysts who were becoming popular for their explanation of mental illness and the effects of the stresses of modern civilization.

However, a third science was emerging: the study of how the brain worked physically, of how perception was processed, and of thinking, or cognition. This study, often called neuroscience or cognitive science, was coming into its own as researchers using a new tool, the electroencephalograph, or EEG, were stimulating different areas of the brain and measuring responses. They were thus creating the first maps of an unknown world—the human brain—pinpointing the motor center, the vision center, and other major regions.

With the coming of World War II, Licklider, like many researchers, found a new assignment. In 1942, Licklider's knowledge of neuroscience was needed by the war effort, and he went to work at the Army Air Corps' newly created Psycho-Acoustics Lab at Harvard University, headed by physicist Leo Beranek (who would later play an important role in developing new computer applications.)

Communications at War

Just as Claude Shannon at about this same time was looking at the physical processing of information as it went from transmitter to receiver (see chapter 7, "Unlocking the Signals), the psycho-acoustics researchers were trying to understand what affected the ability of the human ear, nervous system, and brain to process information coming through a radio receiver or radar display.

Crews of new highly complex war machines (such as the B-29 bomber) were faced with the need to interpret instruments and carry out intricate procedures in a noisy and often highly stressful environment. In this new technology-based warfare, the weakest link in a communications or control system was often the human operator.

The seemingly abstruse realm of psychology and neuroscience was thus becoming as vital as aerodynamics or electronics.

Licklider's particular area of research was how interference and distortion in radio signals affected a listener's ability to correctly interpret speech. Much to his surprise and that of his colleagues, Licklider discovered that while most forms of distortion made speech harder to understand, one particular kind, which he called "peak-clipping," actually improved reception. (In peak-clipping, the consonants ended up being emphasized in relation to the surrounding vowels.) This work also gave Licklider valuable experience in seeing how small things could greatly affect the quality of the interactions between persons and machines.

The Human-Machine Partnership

While at Rochester, Licklider also participated in a study group at the Massachusetts Institute of Technology led by mathematical genius Norbert Wiener, who was in the process of creating the new field of cybernetics, the science of communication and control. Wiener's restless, high-energy mind threw ideas at his colleagues like sparks coming off a Tesla coil. Some of those sparks landed in the receptive mind of Licklider, who through Wiener's circle was coming into contact with the emerging technology of electronic computing and its exciting prospects for the future. Licklider's psychology background allowed him a perspective rather different from the mathematical and engineering training shared by most early computer pioneers.

This perspective could be startling to Licklider's colleagues. As William McGill recalled much later in an interview cited by M. Mitchell Waldrop in his biography of Licklider:

Lick was probably the most gifted intuitive genius I have ever known. Whenever I would finally come to Lick with the mathematical proof of some relation, I'd discover that he already knew it. He hadn't worked it out in detail, he just ... knew it. He could somehow envision the way information flowed, and see relations that people who just manipulated the mathematical symbols could not see. It was so astounding that he became a figure of mystery to all the rest of us. . . .

Cybernetics emphasized the computer as a system that could interact in complex ways with the environment. To this focus, Licklider added an interest in human-computer interaction and communication. He began to see the computer as a sort of "amplifier" for the human mind that would enable people to cope with the tremendous growth in scientific knowledge. Licklider believed that humans and computers could work together to solve problems that neither could successfully tackle alone. The human could supply imagination and intuition, while the computer provided computational "muscle."

Ultimately, according to the title of Licklider's influential 1960 paper, it might be possible to achieve a true "Man-Computer Symbiosis." Just as two organisms in nature can, through symbiosis, cooperate to fulfill each other's needs, humans and a new generation of computers could partner to keep up with the rapidly growing complexity of science and technology.

Professor at MIT

From 1945 to 1950, Licklider held a lecturer position at Harvard University, while also consulting for the U.S. Navy Electronics Laboratory. During the 1950s, Licklider's career blossomed, and he steadily moved up in the scientific ranks. In 1950, Licklider went to the Massachusetts Institute of Technology, where he served as director of its Acoustics Laboratory, while continuing defense-related consulting and serving as an adviser to the Defense Department Research and Development Board and to the predecessor of NASA.

One disappointment for Licklider was his unsuccessful attempt to establish a full-fledged psychology department at MIT that would elevate the concern for what engineers call "human factors." (At the time, psychology at MIT was a section within the economics department.) Resistance from the engineering and "hard science"–oriented community at MIT proved to be too great. Licklider was disappointed, even depressed by this for a time—until he became interested in a new kind of computing.

Interactive Computing

Licklider left MIT in 1957 and went into the private sector as a vice president for engineering psychology at Bolt, Beranek and Newman (BBN), the company that would become famous for pioneering networking technology and was already doing interesting research on communications, vision, and hearing. Licklider's work at BBN gave him, for the first time, direct access to powerful computers, including one of the first minicomputers, the DEC PDP-1.

BBN also gave Licklider his first taste of interactive computing. In traditional mainframe batch processing, a program had to be punched onto cards and given to an operator. Most of the time, some trivial mistake in syntax would result in the program being returned hours later with a printed error message. With the new minicomputer systems, however, hooking a typewriter-like terminal to the computer allowed the programmer to interact directly with the machine, typing in commands or program text. Any errors could be found and fixed in a matter of moments, and the program rerun.

Some even more advanced forms of computer interfaces were starting to appear. The 1950s had seen a growing interest by the military in dealing with the complexity of new systems such as nuclear weapons, ballistic missiles, and air-defense systems. (Licklider attended a conference on air defense problems in the early 1950s.)

The project to build SAGE (Semi-Automatic Ground Environment), a massive computer-controlled air-defense system, would stretch computer technology to its limits and beyond. In particular, SAGE introduced computer interface features that are taken for granted today, such as a video screen display and even a "light gun" that could be touched to the screen to make selections. Although Licklider did not work directly on the SAGE project, he was very familiar with the people in charge of it, and he and other researchers thought it suggested new possibilities for civilian computer users as well.

Time-sharing

In 1962, the federal Advanced Research Projects Agency (ARPA) appointed Licklider to head the Information Processing Techniques Office (IPTO), a new office focusing on leading-edge development in computer science. This position would give Licklider the opportunity to identify the most promising ideas in computing and get them funded.

In addition to the use of interactive terminals, two new ideas were starting to change the way people used computers. The room-filling mainframe computers of the 1950s, besides being very costly, bulky, and greedy consumers of power, were also rather inefficient. The machine could only run one program at a time, which meant that any unneeded memory (an expensive resource) was wasted.

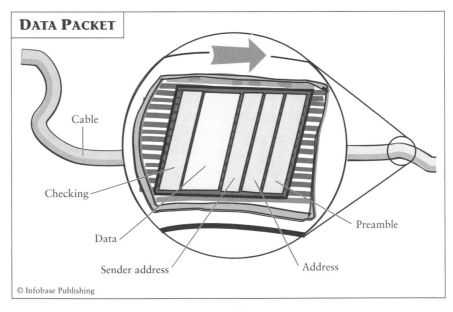

In a computer network, a data packet is like an electronic "envelope" that has forwarding and return addresses as well as a number that is used to check to make sure the data have not been garbled. The data in the packet can represent words, pictures, video, or sound.

The development of new memory control and operating-system hardware made it possible for new computers to load several programs at a time. Each program had its allotted portion of memory for its instructions and data. The processor could then execute a few instructions, switch to the next program, execute some of *its* instructions, and so on. If one program was preoccupied with some relatively slow process (such as reading data or printing a report), the other programs could still run at full speed.

By itself, this multitasking feature primarily served to make computers more efficient and thus able to get more work done per shift. However, a related development, time-sharing, let multiple users each have a portion of the computer's resources. Each user could sit at a separate terminal and run programs or give commands to the machine. Since computers run much faster than people can read or type, each user appeared to have direct access to a responsive machine.

When combined with the development of relatively inexpensive "minicomputers" in the early 1960s, time-sharing made it possible for smaller academic institutions and research labs to buy their own computers. In turn, more people could share in access to the machine, allowing computers to be used for a wider variety of research projects. This spurred an explosion in creativity as young programmers (including the first self-described "hackers" at MIT) began to push the boundaries of the machines' capability, developing such applications as computer graphics, games, and artificial-intelligence applications.

The "Galactic Network"

Licklider used his position at ARPA to funnel federal money to these promising developments. He coined the extravagant name "Galactic Network" to describe his vision of a universal connection that would allow computer users everywhere to share ideas, programs, and resources.

In an interview quoted by Michael and Ronda Hauben in their book *Netizens,* Lawrence Roberts, a later head of IPTO, recalled that *[w]hat I concluded was that we had to do something about communications, and that really, the idea of the galactic network that Lick talked about, probably more than anybody, was something that we had to start seriously thinking about. So in a way networking grew out of Lick's talking about that, although Lick himself could not make anything happen because it was too early when he talked about it. But he did convince me it was important.*

As Roberts notes in an interview in *Netizens,* the early developers of computer time-sharing "were just talking about a network where they could have a compatibility across these systems, and at least do some load sharing, and some program sharing, data sharing that sort of thing." Roberts, however, was inspired by Licklider's Galactic Network idea. He saw that time-sharing was changing not only how people related to the machine but also how they interacted with one another:

As soon as the time-sharing system became usable, these people began to know one another, share a lot of information, and ask of one another, "How do I use this? Where do I find that?" It was really phenomenal to see this computer become a medium that stimulated the formation of a human community.

In turn, Roberts and others helped Licklider widen his own concept of networking. Originally, Licklider had conceived of the Galactic Network as being hosted on a single, giant time-sharing computer system. Roberts and the other developers of ARPANET suggested, however, that networking existing computers was a much more practical and flexible idea.

Fostering Computer Science

Throughout the 1950s and 1960s, Licklider brought together research groups that included in their leadership three of the leading pioneers in artificial intelligence: John McCarthy, Marvin

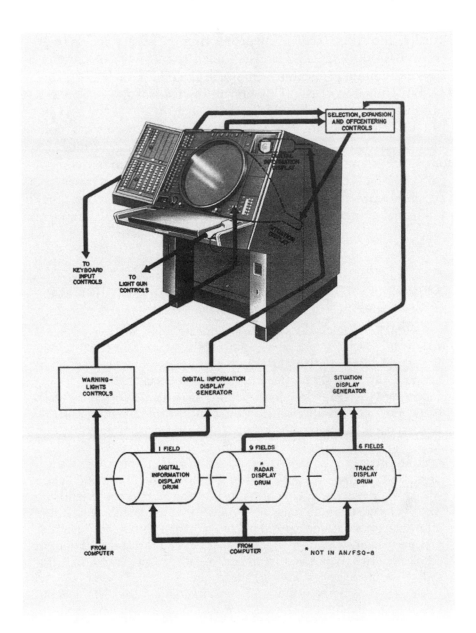

Cold-war air-defense needs spurred the development of high-speed interactive computer systems such as SAGE. This SAGE console included a "light gun" that allowed users to interact directly with images on the screen. (From a SAGE introduction manual)

Minsky, and Allen Newell. By promoting university access to government funding, Licklider also fueled the growth of computer-science graduate programs at major universities such as Carnegie Mellon University, the University of California at Berkeley, Stanford University, and MIT.

In his research activities, Licklider focused his efforts not so much on artificial intelligence as on the development of interactive computer systems that could promote his vision of human-computer symbiosis. He believed that the cooperative efforts of researchers and programmers could develop complex programs more quickly than teams limited to a single agency or corporation. One important

---

OTHER SCIENTISTS: LEONARD KLEINROCK AND LARRY ROBERTS

Although J. C. R. Licklider's vision and management skill played a vital role in the development of computer networking and the Internet, the actual design and implementation of the network owes much to Leonard Kleinrock (1934–) and Lawrence Roberts (1937–).

In a 1961 paper entitled "Information Flow in Large Communication Networks," Kleinrock introduced the concept that would eventually be called packet-switching. Instead of a whole transmission (such as a phone call or stream of computer data) being assigned to a specific circuit, transmissions would be broken up into small pieces, or packets, of data. Because of this, a problem such as a line failure would not break the connection because the system could send the packets by an alternate route. This meant that the system was robust and able to withstand considerable damage, a characteristic that was particularly sought by military planners during the cold war. In 1968, Kleinrock was asked to design a packet-switching system for ARPANET, the ancestor of today's Internet.

Lawrence Roberts worked under Licklider at the MIT Lincoln Lab in the early 1960s. Using Kleinrock's packet-switching idea, he successfully connected a minicomputer at MIT in Boston to a different model in California. In the late 1960s, he joined Kleinrock and another researcher, Robert Taylor, in creating the architecture for ARPANET.

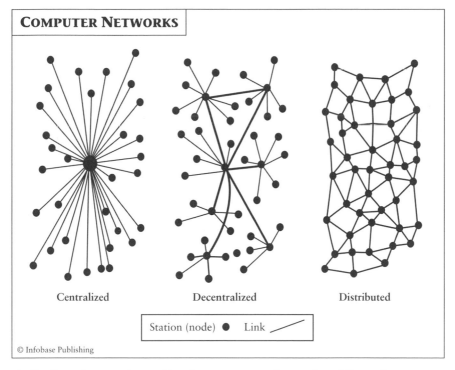

COMPUTER NETWORKS

Centralized   Decentralized   Distributed

Station (node) ●   Link ╱

© Infobase Publishing

A distributed network provides the most protection against failure when a computer "goes down" because there are always alternate paths between any two nodes, or points. A decentralized network represents a good compromise between a more vulnerable centralized network and a more expensive, fully distributed one.

fruit of this effort was the establishment of Project MAC at MIT, the first research center dedicated specifically to cutting-edge topics in computer science.

Following another stint in the private sector (at IBM's Thomas J. Watson Research Center), Licklider returned to Project MAC in 1968 as its director. Licklider would remain at MIT until his retirement in 1985. (Licklider also continued his participation in ARPA and oversaw the official launch of ARPANET, the immediate ancestor of the Internet, in 1975. However, he became disillusioned when ARPA's new director demanded that only research that had a short-term payoff be funded.)

Toward the Internet

Even as late as the 1960s, most people, when asked the purpose of a computer, would have said "data processing." In 1968, however, Licklider and Robert Taylor, however, wrote a paper whose title suggested a quite different application: "The Computer as a Communications Device." Looking back on the progress that had already been made with time-sharing, they noted that

> *[w]e have seen the beginnings of communication through a computer— communication among people at consoles located in the same room or in the same university campus. . . . This kind of communication . . . is beginning to foster cooperation and promote coherence more effectively than do present arrangements for sharing computer programs by exchanging magnetic tape by messenger or mail.*

Looking forward, Licklider and Taylor suggested something that also sounds very familiar today:

> *The collection of people, hardware, and software [with] the multi-access computer together with its local community of users will become a node in a geographically distributed computer network.*

This last statement, conceptually at least, describes what would become the Internet: computers and their users being connected as "nodes" with the ability to communicate worldwide.

Licklider and Roberts also believed that the new online computer systems would create an environment in which

> *we will be able to interact with the richness of living information— not merely in the passive way that we have become accustomed to using books and libraries, but as active participants in an ongoing process, bringing something to it through our interaction with it. . . .*

This was not a bad anticipation of the World Wide Web! The two researchers were not done predicting the future, though. They also anticipated the online "virtual community" (see chapter 10, "Living in Cyberspace") and suggested that online users will form "communities not of common location, but of common interest." At the same time, anticipating the "digital divide," Licklider and Roberts asked themselves whether "being online" would become a privilege or a right. They went on to argue that it must be a right, or the existing lack of equal opportunity in society would only become worse.

I WAS THERE: THE BIRTH OF A NETWORK

It was 1969—exactly 125 years after Samuel Morse had sent his message over the first government-funded telegraph line. Lawrence Kleinrock and his team had connected four computers via telephone lines. Three were in California, at the University of California at San Diego, the Stanford Research Institute in Palo Alto, and the University of California at Santa Barbara. The fourth was at the University of Utah.

Now it was time to test the little network that would be the first step to the Internet. As quoted by author Stephen Segaller, Kleinrock recalls the scene:

> *What was the first message? "What hath God wrought?" Or, "Great step for mankind?" No. All we tried to do was to log on from our host [computer] to their host. Remember—we're engineers.*
>
> *And so we typed in L. And we said [over the phone], "Did you get the L?" And he said "I got the L." Typed the O. "You get the O?" "I got the O." You get the G? Crash! The system failed on the G. A couple hours later, we successfully logged in, did some minimal things, and logged off. That was the first message on the Internet. "Log in, crash."*

A Lasting Legacy

Licklider would not gain the fame of software giants like Bill Gates or even later networking pioneers such as Tim Berners-Lee, inventor of the World Wide Web. However, among the researchers whose collective efforts made today's Internet possible, Licklider is viewed as a key visionary and leader. For example, Michael and Ronda Hauben quote Internet pioneer Larry Roberts as believing that

> *most of the significant advances in computer technology, especially in the systems part of computer science were simply extrapolations of Licklider's vision. They were not really new visions of their own. So he's really the father of it all.*

Perhaps at least as important, though, was Licklider's influence on the creation of modern computer science and computing research. In an interview quoted by the Haubens, Larry Roberts points to Licklider's "influence [in] the production of people in the computer field that are trained, knowledgeable, and capable, and that form the basis for the progress the United States has made in the computer field." Roberts goes on to connect the university effort with the training of the leaders who would create the modern computer industry in all of its many facets.

As for what might have been most important to Licklider himself, M. Mitchell Waldrop quotes the recollections of his children Tracy and Lindy. When they were young and their father was still working in the Pentagon, he would ask them every day upon his return home: "What have you done today that is altruistic, creative, or educational?" The children would then have to review their own day's activities to see if they had done something that had made a difference.

Before his death on June 26, 1990, from complications of asthma, Licklider had certainly made a difference. He also had predicted that by 2000 people around the world would be linked in a global computer network. Licklider received the Franklin Taylor Award of the Society of Engineering Psychologists (1957), served as president of the Acoustical Society of America

(1958), and received the Common Wealth Award for Distinguished Service in 1990.

Chronology

1915	John Carl Robnett Licklider is born on March 11, 1915, in St. Louis, Missouri
1930s	Licklider earns undergraduate degrees in psychology, mathematics, and physics at Washington University, St. Louis; receives master's degree in psychology in 1938
1942	Licklider is awarded a Ph.D. in psychology from the University of Rochester
1943–46	Licklider does research at the Psycho-Acoustics Laboratory at Harvard University
1946–49	Licklider lectures at Harvard
1950–57	Licklider becomes director of the Acoustics Laboratory at MIT; he unsuccessfully attempts to establish a psychology department there
1957–62	Licklider gains experience in the computer field as a vice president for research at Bolt, Beranek and Newman
1960	Licklider publishes a paper on "Man-Computer Symbiosis."
1960s	Licklider helps found computer science laboratories at major universities, including MIT's Project MAC
1962	Licklider becomes director of information-processing research at the Information Processing Techniques Office at ARPA, spurring development of computer networking
1963	Project MAC at MIT begins to develop new time-sharing and interactive computing systems
1968	Licklider and Roberts' paper "The Computer as a Communication Device" foreshadows the Internet

	Licklider returns to MIT and becomes director of Project MAC (until 1970)
1969	First successful computer network linkup results in the establishment of ARPANET
1974–75	Licklider returns to directorship at ARPA Information Processing Technology Office
1975–86	Licklider serves as professor at MIT Laboratory for Computer Science
1990	Licklider dies on June 26, 1990, following complications from an asthma attack

Further Reading

Books

Hauben, Michael, and Ronda Hauben. *Netizens: On the History and Impact of Usenet and the Internet.* Los Alamitos, Calif.: IEEE Computer Society Press, 1997. Also available online. URL: http://www.columbia.edu/~hauben/netbook. Accessed on February 7, 2005.

> Describes the development of early computer networking, including the ARPANET, Usenet, and the Internet; chapters 5 and 6 discuss J. C. R. Licklider's ideas and contributions.

Segaller, Steven. *Nerds 2.0.1: A Brief History of the Internet.* New York: TV Books, 1999.

> Describes the ideas and work leading up to the Internet, along with colorful anecdotes.

Waldrop, M. Mitchell. *The Dream Machine: J. C. Licklider and the Revolution That Made Computing Personal.* New York: Viking, 2001.

> Weaves a biography of Licklider into an intriguing account of the people and ideas that changed the computer world.

Articles

Licklider, J. C. R. "The Computer as Communication Device." *Science and Technology,* April 1968. Available online. URL:

http://www.memex.org/licklider.pdf. Accessed on February 2, 2006.

    This paper not only described what would become the Internet, but it also explored the implications of cyberspace decades before most people would go online.

————. "Man-Computer Symbiosis." *IRE Transactions on Human Factors in Electronics,* vol. HFE-1, pp. 4–11, March 1960. Available online. URL: http://www.memex.org/licklider.pdf. Accessed on February 2, 2006.

    Describes Licklider's vision and strategy for developing systems where humans and computers would cooperate to tackle difficult problems.

"J. C. R. Licklider (1915–1990)" Available online. URL: http://www. columbia.edu/~jrh29/years.html. Accessed on February 7, 2006.

    Summarizes Licklider's career and includes a few quotations about him.

INFORMATION AT OUR FINGERTIPS

TIM BERNERS-LEE AND THE WORLD WIDE WEB

The World Wide Web has been in widespread use for more than a decade. Many young people today cannot remember a time when they could not find just about any information they needed or wanted just by typing a few search words. Google has become in effect the world's largest database system. Web-based businesses such as Amazon.com and eBay can bring almost any item to one's doorstep. Remarkably, it all started because a scientist named Tim Berners-Lee was trying to find a way to keep track of the projects in a huge physics lab.

At Home with Technology

Tim Berners-Lee was born on June 8, 1955, in London, England. Although personal computers were two decades away, Berners-Lee was exposed to computing from an early age because his parents were both mathematicians and programmers for the Manchester University's Mark I, an early mainframe scientific computer. When he was little, hearing his parents talk about their work inspired him to build his own "computer" out of cardboard boxes. He cut slots in them and ran his parents' discarded punched-paper tape as he pretended to operate the machine.

When he was a little older, Tim began to participate in his family's hobby of playing with number games and math puzzles. At a time when his classmates were still learning their multiplication tables, he could talk about imaginary numbers and negative square roots.

In the early 1970s, while attending high school at the Emmanuel School in London, Berners-Lee began to delve deeply into electronics. At the time, microprocessors, or "computer chips," were just starting to become available, and popular electronics magazines began to publish articles suggesting that anyone could build a complete computer that could fit on a desktop. Berners-Lee obtained a microprocessor and connected it to logic circuits that he built himself, and then he connected it to an old television set.

Tim Berners-Lee developed a system of hypertext links to connect information on the growing Internet. The result was the World Wide Web. (© ETH Life, Webjournal of ETH Zurich)

Enquire Within

Computer scientists of the 1960s and 1970s were becoming increasingly aware that computing was just as much about the structure and processing of information as about circuits and devices. Fortunately, Berners-Lee grew up in an environment where information (and ideas about information) was also plentiful. As a little boy who had just learned to read, Berners-Lee had found an old encyclopedia on his parents' bookshelf. It was entitled *Enquire Within upon Everything.* The idea that he could learn whatever he wanted in the pages of a book fascinated young Berners-Lee. As he grew older and his studies progressed, Berners-Lee realized that there was vastly more information in the world than he had imagined, and it was to be found scattered in countless books and articles. Nevertheless, the idea that information could be organized and made accessible would stick with him.

Some time after his encounter with the encyclopedia, the boy asked his father about what he was doing with computers. His father said that he was writing a speech about how computers could be used to link ideas together much in the way the human brain did. Another link on the way to the Web was planted in Tim's mind: Perhaps computers could create the kinds of links between ideas that the little encyclopedia promised but could not really deliver.

The Information Explosion

Berners-Lee also had a strong interest in science, and so he went to Queen's College at Oxford University, where he received a degree in physics with honors in 1976. However, his interests in computers also continued. These increasingly powerful machines had become an essential tool in virtually every field of scientific research. After graduation, Berners-Lee worked for several years in the computer industry. He developed software for a new kind of computer printer and helped develop operating systems, the software that controls the essential functions in any computer system. This experience with fonts, text processing, and computer architecture would also serve Berners-Lee well in his later work on a system for displaying pages on the Web.

In 1980, Berners-Lee returned to the scientific community, becoming an intern at CERN, a giant international physics laboratory in Geneva, Switzerland. Once there, Berners-Lee soon realized that scientists were facing an increasingly daunting information problem.

CERN was one of the world's foremost centers of research in particle physics, and almost 10,000 scientists from around the world had come through the lab on various assignments, often moving from one project to another. Just scheduling meetings and access to time on the shared computer systems was proving to be a daunting task. Even more important was the question of how scientists who spoke different languages and used different computer file formats were going to be able to share equations, charts or graphs, or reports. Without the ability to share their findings, scientists, like inhabitants of the biblical Tower of Babel, would be crippled by their lack of a common language.

Data Dilemmas

CERN tried to use databases to keep track of scientists' work assignments and resources (such as computer hardware and software). Thus, if a particular program or operating system received an upgrade, all the scientists who used it could be notified. A database is basically one or more files containing records, with each record having fields such as scientists' names or room numbers.

The problem was that there was no easy way to link data about one topic to data about another. For example, one could search the employee file and find the record for a scientist, but there was no link from the scientist to the file containing information about computers and their users.

One possible solution was to use what is called a relational database, where records are organized into tables, and the tables can link to each other. Thus the employee file might have an employee ID as one of its fields, while the computer user record might use that same ID, allowing a user to retrieve both the scientist and his or her computer records based on that common field. Relational databases are in common use today, but to construct one, CERN would have to put all of its records into a common format that could be understood by a single database program. Berners-Lee found that there was little possibility of funding or support for such an effort—and besides, he soon decided he wanted to create a much more general and flexible way to link up different kinds of data.

Forging Links

Berners-Lee thought about how people (rather than computers) worked with information. His father had suggested that someday computers might be able to link pieces of information in the way the human mind does. For example, a person might have a memory link such that smelling wood smoke brings back a pleasant image of roasting marshmallows around a campfire as a child. While such links are formed unconsciously, deliberate links are also made to help people manage their growing accumulation of knowledge. For example, writers of encyclopedias such as *Enquire Within* use cross-references to suggest related articles to readers.

As he recounts in his autobiography *Weaving the Web,* Berners-Lee wondered: "Suppose all the information stored on computers everywhere were linked? Suppose I could program my computer to create a space in which anything could be linked with anything?" In other words, suppose a computer could retrieve information not as a database did, but as a brain did?

As Berners-Lee later told *Time* magazine writer Joshua Quittner, he proceeded to write a small program that used links to answer questions about data. Naming it Enquire after his childhood encyclopedia, Berners-Lee used the program to keep "track of all the random associations one comes across in real life and brains are supposed to be so good at remembering but sometimes mine wouldn't."

In the Enquire program, each piece of information (such as the description of a person, computer system, software package, or project) had links to related information. Thus one could go to the record for a scientist and find a link to the description of the computer he or she was using. One could also go the other way, looking at a computer and finding out who used it.

As he notes in his autobiography, Berners-Lee found that creating data links helped him think more clearly about the information involved and about its relationships:

The program was such that I could enter a new piece of knowledge only if I linked it to an existing one. For every link, I had to describe what the relationship was. For example, if a page about Joe was linked to a page about a program, I had to state whether Joe made the program, used it, or whatever. Once told that Joe used a program, Enquire would know, when displaying information about the program, that it was used by Joe. The links worked both ways.

Enquire was an interesting program, but creating all those precise two-way links was labor-intensive. Although some of Berners-Lee's colleagues were impressed by his effort, CERN as an institution was not interested in funding the large-scale system that would be needed to tie together the lab's massive data files. Berners-Lee left CERN in 1980 and spent the next few years working for a variety of software companies on projects such as graphics and instrument-control systems. However, he did not lose his interest in creating linked information systems.

The Open World of Hypertext

In 1984, Berners-Lee was given the opportunity to return to CERN as a permanent staff member, with responsibility for developing a new information system. The lab's management had finally realized that the "information explosion" was only going to get worse, and they were now willing to back a major project to address the problem.

Because the lab's data were in so many different, incompatible file formats, Berners-Lee knew that trying to convert the files and manually set up all the links required for an Enquire-like system would be too expensive and time-consuming. Instead, he would need a way to work with the data in its existing form.

Fortunately, there was already an idea Berners-Lee could draw upon—something called hypertext. The idea of hypertext is that any word or phrase in one document could be set up as a link to take the reader to a related section of text, either within the same document or in a different document or file. Thus, in a hypertext encyclopedia with a sentence reading, "The telegraph played a vital role in the operation of an increasingly complex system of **railroads**," the reader could click on the **railroads** link and go to a page describing the history and development of railroads.

The idea of hypertext actually dated back to a 1945 paper written by Vannevar Bush, who envisaged a mechanical system that could automatically link documents on microfilm. By the 1980s, a growing number of documents were either being scanned into computers or created directly on computer systems, and some experimental hypertext systems were already being created. Berners-Lee, however, needed a more flexible and general system that could deal not with a single document or even a single computer but with networks of computers with different kinds of software and data files.

Linking to the Internet

To create his hypertext system, Berners-Lee took advantage of changes in the way software was being designed. Instead of trying to create a complete, separate hypertext system for each type of computer, he developed a common formatting language that became known as hypertext markup language, or HTML. HTML uses special "tags" written in ordinary text to specify formatting (such as titles or paragraphs) and indicate the text that is to be used as a link to another document.

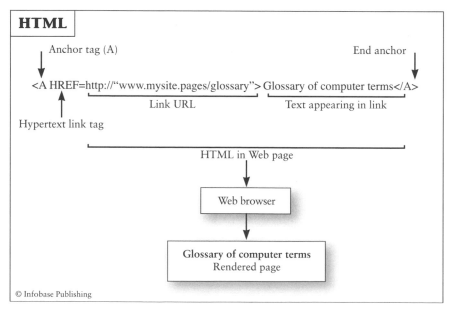

Hypertext markup language (HTML) specifies how text and other elements will appear in a Web browser. Here, text is turned into a link that can take the user to another page.

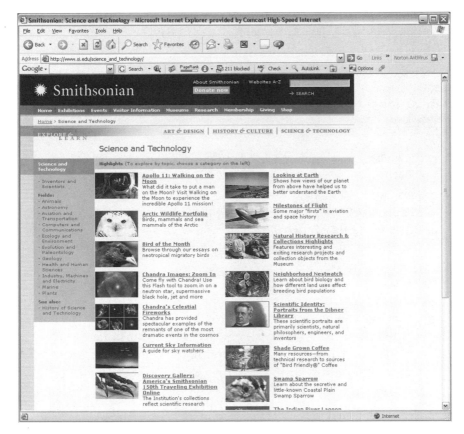

The Web can be a tremendous educational and reference resource. This site for the Smithsonian Institution offers a variety of virtual exhibits.

Rather than developing a separate way of transmitting text from one kind of computer or operating system to another, Berners-Lee took advantage of the fact that there was already a common "information highway" available—the Internet. By the late 1980s, the Internet, though little known to the general public, already linked thousands of computers for universities, research laboratories, software companies, and other technically minded users. Although CERN might have been happy if Berners-Lee had focused on building his hypertext system only on the lab's proprietary network, he realized that this would greatly limit the utility of what he believed

TRENDS: WHO IS USING THE WEB, AND HOW?

The Pew Internet & American Life project issues a variety of reports on the ever-changing use of the Web and other Internet services. As of 2005, some interesting trends that can be gleaned from the project's reports include:

- 72 percent of American adults use the Internet in some form. There are slightly more men (75 percent) than women (69 percent)
- People ages 18–29 have the highest rate of Internet use (84 percent). Only 30 percent of people over age 60 use the Net
- 60 percent of African Americans use the Net—but the gap is closing rapidly
- E-mail (91 percent) and search engines (90 percent) are the most popular Internet applications
- Other popular online activities include getting maps or driving directions (84 percent), researching a consumer product or service (78 percent), and looking for health or medical information (66 percent)
- Less popular activities include reading blogs (27 percent), listening to or viewing digitized broadcasts (29 percent), and participating in online auctions (24 percent)
  However, these percentages still equate to millions of Web users.

to be an extremely valuable tool. Instead, he decided to build on the Internet's existing file transfer and program control facilities, and he developed the Hypertext Transfer Protocol (the familiar HTTP now seen at the start of many Web addresses).

In Berners-Lee's system, each document has a unique address (what is now called a Uniform Resource Locator, or URL). The HTML language specifies the links and formatting in each document. The HTTP system specifies how a program can request a document from an address, whether local or on a computer thousands of miles away.

Finally, two types of programs were needed to complete the system: servers, which can respond to HTTP requests for documents on a given machine, and browsers, which enable a user to request and view documents.

Weaving the Web

In March 1989, Berners-Lee issued an official proposal for linking Internet documents by hypertext. As quoted in his autobiography, Berners-Lee's proposal emphasized that users could "create a common base for communication while allowing each system to maintain its individuality. . . . All you have to do is make up an address for each document or screen in your system and the rest is easy." The ultimate result would be a growing body of accessible, well-linked knowledge that would eventually spread around the world. He therefore called it the World Wide Web.

Although Berners-Lee had designed the system to be easy to implement and use, reaction within CERN was lukewarm. Scientists could see the advantages of such a system, but, naturally, they wanted their time and resources to go to further research, not an extensive effort to revise and link existing documents. Further, there were already two popular systems for making information available over the Internet. One, called WAIS, provided for a way to connect existing databases so they could be searched by Internet users. The other, called Gopher, allowed each Internet site to create menus to allow online access to documents. Berners-Lee's Web was a much more versatile system, but was it worth the extra effort?

When the CERN community gave a noncommital reaction to the Web proposal, Berners-Lee decided that the only thing to do was go ahead and create a system so users could see for themselves just how useful it was. Drawing on his programming skills, the ability to adapt existing software, and the efforts of assistants, Berners-Lee created the first Web server and browser. They then added the necessary addresses and links to provide access to a small but interesting selection of CERN documents. Some of Berners-Lee's colleagues were quite favorably impressed when they saw what the new system could do.

Toward the end of 1991, Berners-Lee started to take the Web "on the road" to show it to users outside of CERN. At a trade show called Hypertext '91 in San Antonio, Texas, he wanted to demonstrate the Web. At the time, however, Internet connections were not particularly common, and Berners-Lee had to string a phone line to a nearby college campus in order to access the Web server at CERN.

By 1992, though, word of the Web was catching on. Programmers began to write Web servers and browsers for other kinds of computers, including the ordinary PCs on peoples' desks. Starting mainly with researchers, computer professionals, and university departments, people began to put Web sites online.

The Web Grows

For its first few years, the Web was mainly a story within the computer world. Most people—even most computer users—did

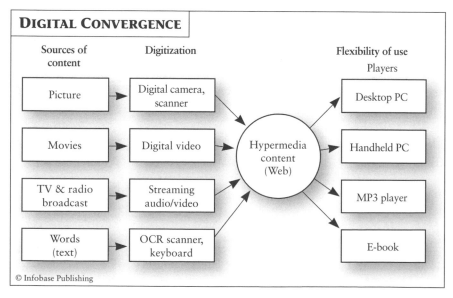

Thanks to digitization and information processing, many formerly separate types of media can be presented in new ways and on devices ranging from desktop PCs to the popular Apple iPod.

not have contact with it. (The most common way for home users to get information and send e-mail was by using services such as CompuServe and America Online.)

What really caused the Web to take off was the development in the mid-1990s of new Web browsers such as Netscape that could display pictures as well as text. (These, in turn, were largely possible because the Web was not proprietary but "open" to any program that could handle the HTML and HTTP specifications.) Today's Web pages can also deliver sound, video, movies, and even digitized television and radio broadcasts.

Having graphics available opened the way for businesses to adapt the techniques of print (and later, TV) advertising to the new medium. The development of "e-commerce" software that allowed users to find and purchase items with just a credit card number and a few clicks brought millions of new users to the Web. In turn, new business models were created, such as eBay, the online auction giant, which made it practical for people to buy and sell goods previously confined to garage sales, and even to create thousands of new home-based businesses.

Berners-Lee had mixed feelings about the Internet boom of the late 1990s. As he notes in his autobiography, the Web "could have faded away, been replaced by a different system. . . ." Once it proved successful, the Web still could "have fragmented, or changed its nature so that it ceased to exist as a universal medium . . . for sharing information." In particular, commercialization of the Web might have meant that some company such as Microsoft or America Online might have created an "improved" version of the Web based on proprietary software and available only to their own customers.

Although some signs of such fragmentation did occur (such as when Microsoft gained the overwhelming share of the Internet browser market and added its own Web-coding features), the Web proved to be too robust and versatile to be "captured" by any one company. Companies such as America Online went from being all-in-one information utilities to providing add-ons to the Internet experience.

Around 2000, an investment boom in Web-based businesses (called dot-coms after the ".com" in Web addresses) turned into a bust when heavily promoted companies could not meet investor expectations. By 2006, however, Web businesses working with more realistic business plans were thriving, and hundreds of millions of people throughout the developed world were downloading music, swapping photos, and exchanging e-mail and instant mes-

---

OTHER INVENTORS: MARC ANDREESSEN

Sometimes the creator of an invention is also its founding entrepreneur—Bell and the telephone are a good example. However, with complex modern technologies, it sometimes takes one or more different people to bring an invention into common use.

Marc Andreessen (1971–) became interested in computers at an early age, though in college he supplemented his computer science studies with a wide range of liberal arts and business interests. An internship at the National Center for Supercomputing Applications (NCSA) in 1993 while still an undergraduate gave Andreessen the opportunity to develop a browser that could add graphics to the text-only Web. The result of the work of Andreessen and his colleagues was a browser called Mosaic, which was offered to users over the Internet at the very attractive price of "free."

In 1994, Andreessen and an older entrepreneur named Jim Clark founded Netscape Corporation. Recruiting many former colleagues from NCSA, the team built a faster, more attractive browser that added the capability to perform secure e-commerce transactions.

Called Netscape Navigator, the browser captured 70 percent of the market in 1994, catching giant Microsoft flatfooted without a Windows browser of its own. In summer 1995, Netscape offered its stock to the public and obtained an amazing $2.3 billion, signaling for many the beginning of the great Internet business boom.

Microsoft eventually brought its formidable resources and its control of Windows to bear, displacing the Netscape browser as market leader. (In recent years, however, faster, more innovative and secure browsers such as Opera and Firefox have made inroads into the domination of Microsoft Internet Explorer). At any rate, Andreessen's development of Mosaic and Navigator jump-started the growth of the Web and demonstrated a successful blend of technical skill and entrepreneurship.

sages. A Web-connected computer had become almost as common an appliance in most American homes as a television set.

Shaping the Future

Unlike inventors such as Morse, Bell, and Edison, Berners-Lee did not start a company to keep control of his invention and to derive financial profits. Rather, he focused on ensuring that the Web maintained a common standard for formatting and accessing documents, allowing the technology to grow without becoming fragmented. In July 1994, Berners-Lee founded the World Wide Web Consortium (W3C). This group brought together many of the people who built the software that runs the Internet and Web, and who have thought about how this new means of communication would or should be used.

Berners-Lee continued to play a key role in the effort to shape the further development of the Web and its interaction with the larger society. In his autobiography, he notes that at the end of the very first World Wide Web conference at CERN, he ended his talk by insisting that "like scientists, people in the Web development community [have] to be ethically and morally aware of what they [are] doing."

When pornographers discovered the Web in the mid-1990s, there were calls for censorship of Web sites—calls that echo today when, for example, the government of China insisted on removing a wide range of "politically sensitive" materials from the search results available to Chinese users, and Google, the world's largest search service, acquiesced. Berners-Lee has always opposed censorship on both technical and philosophical grounds. He was quoted by the *UNESCO Courier* as believing that

> [Censorship] is very difficult to achieve because the Internet allows information to flow in many different ways. . . . In a way, controlling or regulating information is bad for the relationship between a government and the people, and, in the long term, for the stability of the country.

SOCIAL IMPACT: GOVERNING THE WEB

At first, most politicians and opinion leaders were, like the general public, unaware of the significance of the Internet and, particularly, the World Wide Web. However, as the network expanded in the mid- to late 90s and into the new century, a variety of difficult issues arose. The ability of anyone with a few spare dollars a month to create a Web site meant that the fourth grade at PS 101 could have the opportunity to create pages describing their activities and dreams—but it also meant that hate groups such as the Ku Klux Klan, terrorists, and criminals could also use the Web for their own purposes.

The growth of e-commerce, online gambling, and online "adult entertainment" led to a variety of calls for regulating or banning various activities. "Cyber-crime" such as the spreading of computer viruses and identity theft has impacted thousands of users. However, the decentralized architecture of the Net and Web make it very hard to carry out regulation or law enforcement.

There have been calls to redesign the Internet so that data packets could not be sent without the sender being identified. While this would make it easier to track down criminals such as identity thieves or sexual predators, or to detect communications by terrorist groups, it would also mean that the government would potentially know the identities of political dissidents, whistle-blowers, or others whose writings might not be approved of by the authorities. (Indeed, as of early 2006, the revelation of secret wiretaps carried out solely on presidential authority has aroused considerable public concern and debate—and similar techniques can be used to tap or automatically sift through e-mail, instant messages, or Internet-based telephone communications.)

In 1990, former rancher John Perry Barlow and computer entrepreneur Mitch Kapor founded the Electronic Frontier Foundation. Sometimes called the "ACLU of cyberspace," the organization has fought against laws that would subject the Net to censorship or intrusive regulations. Meanwhile, another group, the Electronic Privacy Information Center, seeks greater protection of online users' privacy from government or corporate intrusion.

The future of the Web now seems secure, though the issues to be faced grow more complex as the technology changes. Today the Web is only part of a new world of wireless communications, instant messaging, and the downloading of music and news into portable players. Berners-Lee writes in his autobiography that "The Web is more a social creation than a technical one. I designed it for a social effect—to help people work together—and not as a technical toy."

A Better Web?

In keeping with his vision of the Web as a powerful social tool, Berners-Lee has argued that the existing Web is too passive, since users can only read and react to Web pages but not contribute their own thoughts to them. In recent years, such developments as Weblogs (blogs) and a cooperative knowledge base called Wikipedia have shown how readers can be encouraged to become contributors.

Berners-Lee has also put forth the concept of a "semantic Web," where (more like his original Enquire program) links would not simply connect documents but also describe their relationship. Encoding information about relationship and relevance could allow automatic programs called agents, or "bots," to perform automatically much of the sophisticated online research that now requires specialists. In recent years, HTML has been joined by XML, a language that adds the ability to describe data items and relationships within text.

Berners-Lee has invented a system of knowledge distribution that may be comparable to the printing press in its revolutionary significance. His achievements were quickly recognized by a number of prestigious institutions. Among other honors, Berners-Lee has received the Charles Babbage Award and a MacArthur Fellowship (both in 1998). In 1999, *Time* magazine named Berners-Lee as one of the 100 greatest minds of the 20th century; in 2004, he was knighted by Queen Elizabeth II of Great Britain. In the technical world, Berners-Lee has received top awards from the Association for Computing Machinery and the Institute for Electrical and Electronic Engineering.

There is no doubt that his achievement in allowing the world's information to be woven into increasingly rich forms will shape much of the society and economy of the new century.

Chronology

1945	Vannevar Bush proposes a hypertext system
1955	Tim Berners-Lee is born on June 8 in London
1970s	As a high school student, Berners-Lee builds his own micro-computer
1976	Berners-Lee graduates from Oxford with an honors degree in physics
1980	Berners-Lee goes to work at the CERN physics laboratory as an intern, then works in the software industry
1984	Berners-Lee returns to CERN and becomes responsible for developing new information systems
1989	Berners-Lee issues his World Wide Web proposal at CERN; gets only a limited response
1990	The first Web server comes online at CERN in December
1991	Berners-Lee demonstrates the Web at a hypertext trade show
1991–93	Coordinating a volunteer effort, Berners-Lee refines the HTTP and HTML Web specifications
1994	As the Web grows, Berners-Lee founds the World Wide Web Consortium to set standards
Mid-1990s	Graphical Web browsers bring the Web to home users and consumers
Later 1990s	Investors flock to new Web-based businesses, or "dot-coms"
1999	Berners-Lee becomes a researcher at what will become the Computer Science and Artificial Intelligence Laboratory at MIT *Time* magazine names Berners-Lee as one of the top 100 minds of the 20th century
Early 2000s	Overinflated Web stocks crash in the "dot-bust"
Mid-2000s	Web-based businesses regroup The Web is now almost as ubiquitous as TV

Further Reading

Books

Berners-Lee, Tim. *Weaving the Web*. San Francisco: HarperSan-Francisco, 1999.

> Berners-Lee's autobiography includes much material on the ideas he used in developing the Web and his concerns about its future.

Richards, Sally. *Future Net: The Past, Present, and Future of the Internet as Told by Its Creators and Visionaries*. New York: Wiley, 2002.

> Discusses a variety of issues related to the Internet and World Wide Web, with quotes from numerous key people in the development of the network and e-commerce.

Articles

Anbarasan, Ethirajan. "Tim Berners-Lee: The Web's Brainchild." *UNESCO Courier*, September 2000, p. 46 ff.

> Includes discussion of the international implications of the World Wide Web.

Quittner, Joshua. "Network Designer Tim Berners-Lee." *Time*, 29 March 1999, p. 192 ff.

> Summarizes Berners-Lee's achievements and why he was selected as one of the top 100 minds of the 20th century.

Web Sites

Electronic Frontier Foundation. URL: http://www.eff.org. Accessed on February 1, 2006.

> Advocacy group that argues against censorship and intrusive regulation of the Internet.

Electronic Privacy Information Center. URL: http://epic.org. Accessed on February 1, 2006.

> Provides extensive news and resources about threats to online privacy, including misuse of consumer information by businesses.

Pew Internet and American Life. URL: http://www.pewinternet.org. Accessed on February 5, 2006.

> A division of the Pew Research Center, this project does extensive research and provides important reports on the changing use of the Web and Internet, including how different demographic groups use

the Net and how technology is changing entertainment, the news, and social life.

Tim Berners-Lee. URL: http://www.w3.org/People/Berners-Lee. Accessed on August 28, 2006.

Home page including links to Berners-Lee's talks, articles, interviews, and technical papers.

World Wide Web Consortium. URL: http://www.w3.org. Accessed on February 3, 2005.

Develops policies, guidelines, tools and software; "leading the Web to its full potential."

10
LIVING IN CYBERSPACE

HOWARD RHEINGOLD AND VIRTUAL COMMUNITIES

Chat rooms, online conferences, multiplayer games in virtual worlds—these are all places that exist not in physical space but in what science-fiction writer William Gibson called "cyberspace." First with primitive online bulletin boards in the 1980s and later in elaborate graphical settings via the Internet, people have been getting together online for almost three decades to discuss just about any topic, to play games, to flirt—to do just about anything that does not require a physical presence. Indeed, for many participants, their online life may seem more real than their "real" one.

A writer named Howard Rheingold has spent a long and varied career exploring cyberspace, chronicling the birth and growing pains of virtual communities, and observing new forms of communication and social interaction from the streets of Tokyo to the electronically organized political movements of the 21st century.

Tools for Thought

Rheingold was born on July 17, 1947, in Phoenix, Arizona, where he grew up. He was educated at Reed College in Portland, Oregon, from 1964 to 1968. Young Rheingold imbibed deeply of the hippie subculture, with its interest in the byways of consciousness and the writings of Eastern spiritual teachers. (His senior thesis was entitled: "What Life Can Compare with This? Sitting Alone at the

Howard Rheingold's writings focus on the development of new forms of community as a result of new communications technologies, ranging from chat rooms to "smart mobs" connected by text messaging. (Courtesy of Howard Rheingold)

Window, I Watch the Flowers Bloom, the Leaves Fall, the Seasons Come and Go."

Rheingold has lived and worked for most of his life in the San Francisco Bay Area. A professional writer since the age of 23, Rheingold spent the 1970s and early 1980s in writing about "consciousness studies" at the Institute of Noetic Sciences in Petaluma, California, and exploring the new ideas in computer interfacing being developed at the Xerox PARC lab in Palo Alto, California (home of the original mouse-and-windows interface).

Rheingold's exploration of computer technology focused not on its computational prowess but on the possibilities it opened for exercising creativity and imagination. His book *Tools for Thought* (originally published in 1985 and revised in 2000) combined accounts of early computer pioneers such as Charles Babbage with reports on modern computer scientists and inventors such as Douglas Engelbart (inventor of the mouse) and Ted Nelson (developer of a hypertext system called Xanadu) who were changing the way people interacted with computers and organized ideas. At a time when the word *Internet* was unknown to the general public, Rheingold suggested that computer-mediated communications had tremendous potential for creating new forms of community. This focus on tools reflected the technological side of the "hippie" movement, typified by Stewart Brand's *Whole Earth Catalog,* which Rheingold would revise in 1994.

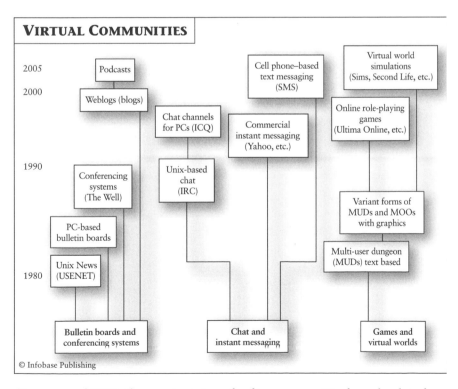

VIRTUAL COMMUNITIES

© Infobase Publishing

Since around 1980, three major types of online communities have developed: bulletin boards, chat/messaging systems, and virtual worlds.

Another track that Rheingold pursued in the 1980s was the exploration of consciousness and cognitive psychology. His books in this area include *Higher Creativity* (written with Willis Harman, 1984), *The Cognitive Connections* (written with Howard Levine, 1986) and *Exploring the World of Lucid Dreaming* (written with Stephen LaBerge, 1990).

Plunging into Cyberspace

Even as he was beginning to write about the computer revolution, Rheingold was becoming increasingly involved in it personally. As he recalled later in a speech, Rheingold bought his first personal computer, mainly because he thought word processing would make his work as a writer easier. In 1983, he bought a modem (which at the time cost $500 and ran at the barely adequate speed of 1200 baud, or bits per second). On his Web site, Howard Rheingold says that he "fell into the computer realm from the typewriter dimension, then plugged his computer into his telephone and got sucked into the net." He was soon intrigued by the "rich ecology of the thousands of PC bulletin board systems that ran off single telephone lines in peoples' bedrooms." Interacting with these often tiny cyberspace villages helped Rheingold explore his developing ideas about the nature and significance of virtual communities.

Virtual Communities

In 1985, Rheingold joined The WELL (Whole Earth 'Lectronic Link), a unique and remarkably persistent community that began as an unlikely meeting place of Deadheads (Grateful Dead fans) and computer hackers. Compared to most bulletin boards, The WELL was more like the virtual equivalent of the cosmopolitan San Francisco Bay Area. Later, Rheingold recalled that

In the fifteen years since I joined The WELL, I've contributed to dozens of . . . fund-raising and support activities. I've sat by the

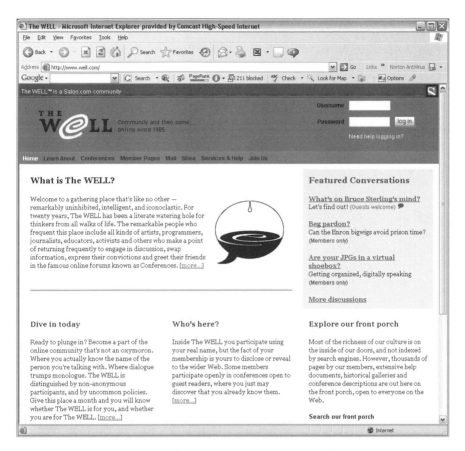

The WELL, a computer conferencing system founded in the mid-1980s, is probably the oldest-existing "virtual community"—and an early inspiration for Howard Rheingold's work. This is its home page.

bedside of a dying, lonely woman, who would have died alone if it had not been for people she had previously known only as words on a screen. I've danced at four weddings of people who met online. I've attended four funerals, and spoke at two of them.

Suggesting that the question of whether online communities are "real" communities may be missing the point, Rheingold chronicled the romances, feuds ("flame wars"), and growing pains that made The WELL seem much like a small town or perhaps an artist's colony that just happened to be in cyberspace.

PARALLELS: ONLINE GAMES

The early text-based online games such as MUDs (multiuser dungeons) of the 1980s reflected a new type of role-playing game first popularized by Dungeons and Dragons. The ability to create characters and, indeed, assume an alternate identity was almost intoxicating to many players. Players sometimes formed lasting relationships (or messily broke up).

Today the descendant of those early games is the "massively multiplayer online game" that began in the late 1990s with titles such as *Ultima Online* and *Everquest.* Today other popular online games include *Asheron's Call* and *City of Heroes.* Unlike these fantasy or superhero-based worlds, games such as *The Sims* and *Second Life* offer a simulated real-world setting.

Although these games have different flavors and features, they have some important features in common. The player can create one or more "avatars," or characters, that represent the player in the game world. (This character can be quite different from the player's real-world identity, such as being of different ethnicity, age, gender, or even species.) Depending on the game, avatars engage in a variety of activities, including quests and battles but also such mundane activities as building and furnishing a house or operating a store.

Because players often spend many hours a week in the game world, a considerable amount of time and effort goes into developing characters and obtaining possessions. As a result, some players are willing to buy or sell in-game goods using real-world money, creating a sort of parallel economy that may eventually attract the attention of tax authorities and regulators.

The immersive graphics and open-ended nature of the game world makes it a virtual reality. The "guilds" and other organizations in which player-characters participate could be considered a type of virtual community, but how lasting or relevant it might be is an open question.

The sum and evaluation of Rheingold's online experiences can be found in what is perhaps Rheingold's most seminal book, *The Virtual Community* (1993 and revised in 2000), which represents his tour as both participant and observer through the online meeting places that had begun to function as communities. In addition to The WELL, Rheingold also explored MUDs (multiuser dungeons) and other elaborate online fantasy role-playing games, NetNews (also called Usenet) groups, chat rooms, and other forms of online interaction. Looking toward a future where powerful graphics capabilities would make the online world even more compelling, in 1991 Rheingold's book *Virtual Reality* introduced the immersive technology that was being pioneered by researchers such as Jaron Lanier. At the time, this technology was little known, and Rheingold's first-hand accounts of the work in VR labs made him a popular speaker at conferences.

Toward the end of the 1990s, much conferencing activity became Web-based, and a new phenomenon, the Weblog (or blog) allowed people to maintain a sort of interactive diary. Rheingold's use of his own Web site for communicating his thoughts pretty much anticipates the blog.

"Smart Mobs"

Around 1999, Rheingold started noticing the emergence of a different kind of virtual community—a mobile, highly flexible, and adaptive one. While on a trip to Tokyo, he noticed that many young people were reading tiny screens on their cell phones and typing text rather than talking. This "text-messaging" technology soon caught on in the United States and Europe as well.

In his book *Smart Mobs* (2002), Rheingold gives examples of groups of teenagers coordinating their activities by sending each other text messages on their cell phones. (The Japanese gave them the whimsical name of "thumb tribes.") In 1999, in the "Battle of Seattle," anti–World Trade Organization protesters used mobile communications and Web sites to rapidly shift and "swarm" their objectives, often outflanking police who relied upon traditional communications and chains of command. The "people power" revolution in the Philippines in 2000

CONNECTIONS: FINDING FRIENDS

In the mid-2000s, one of the hottest online applications is turning out to be Web-based services that keep people in touch with their friends, or help them find lost friends or classmates. For example, MySpace.com is very popular with young people, with about 49 million users by the end of 2005. Another service, Facebook.com, is particularly popular with college students.

Although social networking services have different features and somewhat different target audiences, they basically work as follows. Each user submits a "profile" of themselves, including a description, list of interests (such as favorite music and movies), and a photo. (Facebook members are limited to linking to students in the same school, but MySpace has no geographical limitation.) Once signed up, a user can search for other users who share the same interests. Users can also indicate that other users are friends and indicate how they met. In Facebook, a "social time line" can then be displayed, summarizing how and when a person met each friend. In addition to groups of friends, users can form groups and schedule parties and meetings. There are also a variety of ways to send messages to keep in touch.

As with all human activities, online social networks have had their share of problems. Some college police departments have used Facebook entries to discover activities such as underage drinking. Some high schools have blocked their students from services such as Facebook and MySpace because of their alleged use to organize "hate groups" or other disruptive activities. (With younger students, parents and Internet watchdog groups have also warned about possible use by online sexual predators with bogus profiles.)

San Francisco Chronicle writer Reyan Harmanci quotes Howard Rheingold as not being surprised by the popularity of social networking sites, noting that "People's behavior will change with technology. I know very few young people who can't type out a text message on their phone with one thumb, for instance. . . . It's a Facebook generation."

showed this phenomenon on an even larger scale, with text message–coordinated demonstrations by more than 1 million people, leading to the overthrow of the government of President Joseph Estrada.

In the book, Rheingold defines "smart mobs" as groups of people who "are able to act in concert even if they don't know each other." Rheingold believes that the combination of mobile and network technology may be creating a social revolution as important as that triggered by the PC in the 1980s and the Internet in the 1990s. Already, according to the book, this rapidly evolving technology is changing "the way people meet, mate, work, [conduct] war, buy, sell, govern, and create." Further, Rheingold notes that this is all happening in the context of a future where appliances, cars, even whole buildings will have built-in computers and wireless connections, exchanging a tremendous amount of information about activities and locations.

As he points out in an interview with *Reason* magazine, this new world of "smart" and connected people and things is not without drawbacks and potential problems: "We're entering a world in which the complexity of the devices and the system of interconnecting devices is beyond our capability to easily understand." Rheingold, like many others who write about the connected world, sees its potential for robbing people of their privacy and opening them to insidious forms of attack. (After all, the same system that knows where people are at all times and can dispatch emergency help might also be used to track the movements of political dissidents.) Thus, Rheingold tells the *Reason* interviewer that "With much of what I'm writing about there's an upside and a downside, and it's hard to tell which ones are going to prevail. I think it's not either/or but both/and."

Prolific Writer

Virtual communities and computer technology have not been Rheingold's only interests. Like many writers, he has been fascinated by the tools of his own trade—words. Together with coauthor Howard Levine, the book *Talking Tech: A Conversational Guide to Science and Technology* describes how 70 scientific terms have become a part of common usage—and gives guidance on how to use them correctly. Rheingold also explores the less tangible realms of language in *They*

SOCIAL IMPACT: COMMUNITIES OF COOPERATION

Several forms of online cooperation that have become popular in recent years can express the power of cooperative effort to create resources of lasting value. One is the "open-source" movement whose most successful fruit is probably the Linux operating system. A modern computer-operating system and its related utilities make up one of the most complicated products humans have ever devised. Traditionally, development of such software has required the kind of commitment of time and money only available to a major corporation or academic institution.

With Linux, however, its inventor Linus Torvalds created a minimal version of the "core" of the system (together with utilities from existing open-source projects), and then enlisted volunteers to create whatever extensions they thought would be useful and appropriate. A sort of filtering process then evaluates the quality of each submission and decides when it is ready to be incorporated in the next release of the system.

The system called Wikipedia (*wiki* is a Hawaiian word meaning "quick") applies the open-source idea to creating a new kind of encyclopedia. Anyone can create, revise, or add to any of hundreds of thousands of articles. Through a process of community discussion, the articles are gradually refined and inaccuracies removed. The same idea has been applied to creating Wikis for private use by organizations.

There are a number of other cooperative efforts that express varying degrees of organization and purpose. A SETI (Search for Extraterrestrial Intelligence) effort called SETI @Home has enlisted PC users to install programs that can process batches of radio telescope data for signs of alien signals without disturbing the user's main work. Similarly, in 2006, NASA asked for volunteers to visually examine photos that may show tiny bits of comet material captured and returned by a space probe.

While none of these efforts is in itself a coherent virtual community, the creation of such projects (and the willingness of people to participate in them) is perhaps evidence of a growing ability of people to create social structures in cyberspace.

Have a Word for It: A Lighthearted Lexicon of Untranslatable Words and Phrases, where he succeeds in describing about 200 images or ideas that express fundamental human concerns but do not quite correspond to any English words. Clearly, the ability to explore and stretch the limits of language has served Rheingold well in his attempt to describe new ways of communication and community.

Community Builder

Rheingold has not just written extensively about virtual communities and new forms of communication; he has also helped create them. Rheingold ventured into Web publishing in 1994, helping

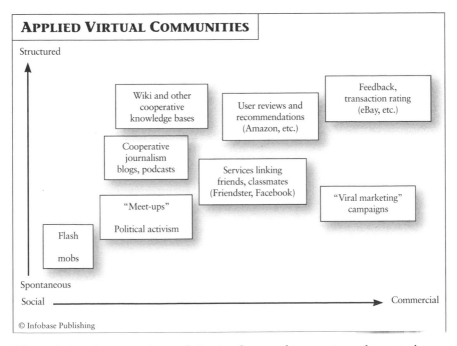

Ideas of virtual community are being implemented in a variety of ways today. This chart plots some types of virtual communities according to whether they are primarily social or commercial in purpose, and the degree to which they form spontaneously or are structured.

design and serve as the first executive editor of *HotWired,* which he soon quit (according to his Web page) "because I wanted something more like a jam session than a magazine."

In March 1996, Rheingold launched Electric Minds, an innovative company that tried to offer virtual community-building services while attracting enough revenue from contract work and advertising to become self-sustaining and profitable in about three years. He received financing from the venture capital firm Softbank. The Electric Minds site was named one of the best Web sites of 1996 by *Time* magazine, but the company ran out of money by that July. According to an interview with the online journal *Mindjack,* Rheingold believes that what he learned from the experience is that venture capitalists who want a quick and large return on the investment "were not a healthy way to grow a social enterprise." Looking back, Rheingold suggests that he should have focused on the basic conferencing software and social features instead of expensive professional design.

Although Rheingold's work is serious and thoughtful, no account of him would be complete without mentioning his playful, trickster-like approach to life and his collection of colorfully painted shoes. As he told Dan Richards of *Mindjack,* "I've always dressed funny, but never really advertised it. Then I started working the press, figured out what they wanted and how it could draw attention to my writing, and by the time Electric Minds was launched, I had my black belt in media self-promotion."

Around the same time, Rheingold also played an important part in creating The River, an online conferencing community similar in many ways to The WELL but owned by its members and run cooperatively.

Rheingold then started a more modest effort, Rheingold Associates, which, according to its Web site, "helps commercial, educational, and nonprofit enterprises build online social networks and knowledge communities." Rheingold also manages the Brainstorms Community, a private Web-conferencing community that allows for thoughtful discussions about a variety of topics.

According to Rheingold and coauthor Lisa Kimball, some of the benefits of creating such communities include the ability to get essential knowledge to the community in times of emergency, to connect people who might ordinarily be divided by geography or interests, to "amplify innovation," and to "create a community memory" that prevents important ideas from getting lost. Rheingold continues to both create and write about new virtual communities.

Rheingold's writings have garnered a variety of awards. In 2003, *Utne* magazine gave an Independent Press award for a blog based on *Smart Mobs*. That year, Rheingold also gave the keynote speech for the annual Webby Awards for Web site design.

Chronology

1947	Howard Rheingold is born on July 17 in Phoenix, Arizona
1964–68	Rheingold attends Reed College
1970s	Rheingold begins his writing career
1980s	Rheingold studies and writes about consciousness and technology
	Computer users connect to online bulletin boards
	Text-based multiplayer games (MUDs) begin
1983	Rheingold gets a modem and goes online
1985	Rheingold publishes *Tools for Thought*
	The WELL is founded
1991	Rheingold publishes *The Virtual Community*
1994	Rheingold creates the HotWired Web site
1996	Rheingold launches the Electric Minds site, but it runs out of money after a few months
1999–2000	Text-messaging is used to coordinate large-scale political protests
2002	Rheingold publishes *Smart Mobs,* a study of the emerging mobile text-messaging culture
2004	Social-networking sites such as Facebook and MySpace become popular

Further Reading

Books

Hafner, Katie. *The Well: A Story of Love, Death & Real Life in the Seminal Online Community*. New York: Carol & Graf, 2001.
> Describes the growth (and growing pains) of a text-based conferencing system that became one of the oldest virtual communities.

Rheingold, Howard. *Tools for Thought: The History and Future of Mind-Expanding Technology*. 2nd Rev. ed. MIT Press, 2000.

———. *The Virtual Community: Homesteading on the Electronic Frontier*. Rev. ed. MIT Press, 2000. (The first edition is also available online. URL: http://www.rheingold.com/vc/book.)

Articles

Harmanci, Reyhan. "Online Networking Clicks among Friends." *San Francisco Chronicle*, October 23, 2005, A-1. Also available online. URL: http://www.sfgate.com (search).
> Describes Facebook and MySpace, social-networking sites that are particularly popular with young people.

Kimball, Lisa, and Howard Rheingold. "How Online Social Networks Benefit Organizations." Available online. URL: http://www.rheingold.com/Associates/onlinenetworks.html. Accessed on February 5, 2006.
> Describes the benefits of virtual community building for businesses and other organizations.

Rheingold, Howard. "Community Development in the Cybersociety of the Future." BBC Online. Available online. URL: http://www.partnerships.org.uk/bol/howard.htm. Accessed on November 3, 2002.

Richards, Dan. "The Mind of Howard Rheingold." *Mindjack* 1 (September 15, 1999). Available online. URL: http://www.mindjack.com/interviews/howard1.html. Accessed on August 28, 2006.
> Two-part interview with Rheingold in an online magazine.

Walker, Jesse. "Is That a Computer in Your Pants?: Cyberculture Chronicler Howard Rheingold on Smart Mobs, Smart Environments, and Smart Choices in an Age of Connectivity." *Reason*, April 2003, pp. 36–42.

Wide-ranging interview in which Howard Rheingold expounds on trends in networking and smart devices and their implications.

Web Sites

Howard Rheingold. URL: http://www.rheingold.com. Accessed on January 12, 2006.
  Provides a bit of background, plus links to Rheingold's writings and activities, including the text of his books *The Virtual Community* and *Tools for Thought*.
The WELL. URL: http://www.well.com. Accessed on February 1, 2006.
  This San Francisco Bay Area–based conferencing system was founded in 1985 and has many regular participants who engage in ongoing discussions on dozens of topics as well as participating in occasional "real-world" social events.

CHRONOLOGY

1844	Samuel Morse sends "What hath God wrought?" message on the first regular telegraph line, from Washington, D.C., to Baltimore
1861	The transatlantic telegraph is completed
1861–65	The U.S. Civil War increases the need for military and civilian communications
1864	James Maxwell develops a comprehensive theory of electromagnetic waves that predicts the possibility of radio
1866	The first successful transatlantic telegraph cable is completed
1870s	Thomas Edison and Alexander Graham Bell work on "multiplex" telegraphs to send multiple messages
1876	Bell demonstrates the telephone at the Centennial Exposition in Philadelphia
1877	Edison invents the phonograph
1887	Heinrich Hertz demonstrates the existence of radio waves
1892	Automatic telephone switches and dial telephones are introduced
1893	Edison introduces the Kinetoscope, a primitive movie projector
1895	Edison and the Lumière brothers show films in theaters
1897	Joseph J. Thomson discovers the electron; the cathode-ray tube is invented
1899	Marconi uses his wireless system to report yacht races and other news

1901	Marconi sends the first transatlantic wireless signal
1904	John Fleming builds the first vacuum tube to detect radio signals
1906	Lee De Forest invents the triode (audion) amplifier tube
1909	Wireless, now common on ships, is used for the first sea rescue
1912	Edwin Armstrong invents the regeneration, or feedback, circuit, greatly amplifying radio waves
1915	Transcontinental telephone service begins
	The Birth of a Nation pioneers new movie camera techniques
1920s	Armstrong's "superheterodyne" makes radio receivers more sensitive
	Sound is added to the movies
	Commercial radio broadcasting begins
	Vacuum tube technology boosts radios and phonographs
	Philo Farnsworth begins his television experiments
1930s	Radio broadcasting booms despite the Great Depression
	Edwin Armstrong demonstrates FM, but its commercial development is stifled
	Limited television broadcasting begins in the United States, Britain, and Germany
1940s	World War II greatly spurs electronics development, including digital computers
	Long-playing (LP) and 45 rpm records are introduced toward the end of the decade
1948	Claude Shannon publishes a groundbreaking paper on information and communications theory
1950s	Records and radio promote rock and roll
	Television enters millions of American households
	Mainframe computers increase in power

1960s	Minicomputers and time-sharing bring computing to universities and labs
	FM becomes the premier medium for music broadcasting
1969	First successful test of ARPANET computer network
1970s	Telephone systems become increasingly computerized
1980s	AT&T's telephone monopoly is broken up by a federal court
	Compact disks (CDs) replace vinyl records
	Computerized special effects become common in movies
	Talk radio becomes popular
	Computer users begin to post messages on electronic bulletin boards
	Information services such as America Online become popular
1990s	Cordless and cell phone use becomes widespread
1991	Tim Berners-Lee introduces the World Wide Web
1995	Graphical browsers introduce the Web to PC users
2000	Many Web-based business fail in "dot.com" crash
2000s	Text messaging becomes popular among youths; "smart mob" social phenomenon is studied by Howard Rheingold
	MP3 players and the iPod provide new ways to enjoy music on the go
	Satellite radio becomes popular
	Television programs can be downloaded from the Internet

# GLOSSARY

45 rpm speed used for small records, usually containing a single song per side

alternating current current that reverses direction many times a second

amplifier device that strengthens a sound or signal

amplitude modulation (AM) transmitting a signal by varying the strength of a radio wave

anode positive electrode that attracts electrons

ARPA the Advanced Research Projects Agency of the U.S. Defense Department (sometimes called DARPA)

ARPANET experimental computer network created with Pentagon funding in the late 1960s; it gradually entered the public domain as the Internet

artificial intelligence (AI) the attempt to create behavior in computers that seems to require intelligence, learning, adaptability, or creativity

bandwidth capacity of a channel to carry information; often expressed in bits

capacitance tendency of electricity to accumulate or be stored

cathode negative electrode that gives off electrons

cathode-ray tube device that generates streams of electrons that make chemical dots (phosphors) selectively glow; the basis for television

circuit path through which electricity flows from a source, usually through various devices, and then usually back to the source

circuit-switching "classic" method of communications where each pair of callers has a separate, dedicated circuit

compact disk (CD) coated disk on which sound is digitally stored and read using a laser; replaced vinyl records in the 1980s

conductor a material (such as copper) through which electricity can flow freely

cybernetics the study of control and interaction of machines; developed by Norbert Wiener

database an organized collection of information in files, records, and fields

diaphragm a thin, stretched membrane that can vibrate

digital convergence the ability to digitally manipulate formerly separate types of media (such as graphics, sound, and video) and to make them available over the Internet

digital divide a situation in which some groups (such as the poor, minorities, or the elderly) may have less access to the Internet and computer technology

digitization the representation of a signal (such as sound) or an image by numeric data that can be manipulated using a computer

direct current current that flows constantly in one direction

electrode a connector that provides electric current to a device

electromagnetic wave a wave of electrical and magnetic energy (such as a radio wave) that can pass through space

electromagnetism the force of which electricity and magnetism are two interchangeable aspects

electron a tiny, negatively charged particle; the carrier of electricity

electronics the study and control of the flow of electrons

frequency the number of electromagnetic waves that pass a point in one second

frequency modulation (FM) transmitting a signal by varying the frequency of radio waves

high fidelity (hi-fi) accurate reproduction of sound; a goal of many hobbyists starting in the 1940s

HTML (hypertext markup language) a language that specifies how Web pages will be formatted and linked

HTTP (hypertext transmission protocol) a set of procedures used to request Web pages from a server

hypertext system in which documents (or sections of documents) include links to related material

induction causing a current to flow, such as by a moving magnetic field

information   in communications, the meaningful contents of a signal
information theory   the study of the interaction of information with its transmission channel and receiver, and ways to correct errors in transmission
insulator   a material (such as rubber) that keeps electricity from flowing
integrated circuit   a silicon "chip" containing millions of individual electronic components
Internet   the worldwide linked system of computer networks using a common communications protocol
internet protocol (IP)   the standard procedures for routing data between addresses on the Internet
laser   a device producing a beam of light in which all waves have the same frequency and are synchronized
LCD (liquid crystal display)   a screen that uses layers of a liquid crystal solution that can selectively block light when a current passes through it. LCDs are used in laptop computers and flat-panel monitors and TVs
LP   a long-playing (vinyl) phonograph record
microphone   device that converts sound waves to an electrical signal
multimedia   the combining of a variety of sound and visual media in a single product
neuroscience   the study of nerve transmission, brain connections, and information processing in organisms
noise   distortion of a signal due to interference or natural causes
oscillation   rapid, back-and-forth, wavelike motion
packet   a "chunk" of data that includes addressing information
packet-switching   communications coordinated through separately routed data packets that are reassembled at the destination
persistence of vision   the brain's lag in perceiving a change in a visual image, which can be exploited to create moving pictures
phosphor   a spot on a television tube that glows when struck by an electron beam
rectifier   device that changes an alternating current into a direct current
redundancy   duplicate information that can be used to correct communications errors
regeneration   the amplification of a radio signal by feeding it back into the receiver

repeater   device that receives a signal and generates a new, stronger copy

resistance   the tendency to oppose the flow of electricity

resonance   sympathetic vibration, as when a receiver picks up a frequency to which it is tuned

semantic Web   Tim Berner-Lee's concept of Web pages that include codes that can help convey the meaning of their contents

semiconductor   a material that is neither a good conductor nor a good insulator

smart mobs   spontaneously organized groups of people who are constantly in touch through text messaging with cell phones

social networking   online services that bring together friends, classmates, or other people with common interests

static electricity   electricity that discharges suddenly rather than flowing continuously in a current

superheterodyne   combining of the received signal with another signal to create a lower-frequency signal that is easier to manipulate

text messaging   typing short messages, usually on cell phones or handheld computers

transistor   a solid-state device made from semiconducting materials that can perform functions (such as amplification) previously handled by vacuum tubes

URL (uniform resource locator)   a unique address specifying the location of a Web page

virtual community   a social group that interacts primarily through an online service

virtual reality   the creation of a simulated world using immersive computer graphics, sound, and touch (tactile feedback)

wavelength   the distance from one wave peak or trough and the next

Web browser   program used to request and view pages on the World Wide Web

Web server   program that responds to requests for Web pages and processes user interaction with online forms and other features

World Wide Web   the system of linked text (and later, graphics and multimedia) developed by Tim Berners-Lee in the early 1990s

XML   a language for specifying the structure and relationships of data in databases and Web pages

FURTHER RESOURCES

Books

Blanchard, Margaret A., ed. *History of the Mass Media in the United States*. Chicago: Fitzroy Dearborn, 1998.

> A copious reference work on every aspect of the broadcast mass media, including technology, the development of the broadcast profession, and social impact.

Clarke, Arthur C. *How the World Was One: Beyond the Global Village*. New York: Bantam Books, 1992.

> Describes how the development of communications technology has brought people together and transformed societies.

Hafner, Katie, and Matthew Lyon. *Where Wizards Stay up Late: The Origins of the Internet*. New York: Simon & Schuster, 1996.

> A classic account of the lives and work of networking pioneers such as J. C. R. Licklider, Lawrence Roberts, Robert Kahn, and Vinton Cerf.

Henderson, Harry. *A to Z of Computer Scientists*. New York: Facts On File, 2003.

> Biographical dictionary presenting the lives of more than 100 computer scientists and inventors, many of whom contributed to the development of the Internet and World Wide Web.

———. *Internet Predators* (Library in a Book). New York: Facts On File, 2005.

> A guide to the struggle to protect the World Wide Web from criminal predators and fraud while preserving the medium's freedom. Includes a research guide and extensive bibliographies.

———. *Power of the News Media* (Library in a Book). New York: Facts On File, 2004.

> A guide and reference handbook to both print and broadcast media; includes a research guide and extensive bibliographies.

Lubar, Stephen. *InfoCulture: The Smithsonian Book of Information Age Inventions*. Boston: Houghton Mifflin, 1993.

An account of the development of communications and information processing, combining a vivid narrative with numerous illustrations from the Smithsonian exhibit of the same name.

Lewis, Tom. *Empire of the Air: The Men Who Made Radio*. New York: HarperCollins, 1991.

A fascinating narrative history and biography of radio pioneers including Lee De Forest, Edwin Armstrong, and David Sarnoff. (It was also made into a television documentary.)

Segaller, Steven. *Nerds 2.0.1: A Brief History of the Internet*. New York: TV Books, 1999.

Describes the development of the Internet through the eyes and voices of the people who created it.

Internet Resources

Center for Media Literacy. URL: http://www.medialit.org. Accessed on January 15, 2006.

Provides resources for parents, children, and teachers to learn how to become better, more critical users of mass media.

ClickZ Stats. URL: http://www.clickz.com/stats. Accessed on February 9, 2006.

Provides numerous statistics and trend reports on Web marketing, e-commerce, advertising, and new applications.

Electronic Frontier Foundation. URL: http://www.eff.org. Accessed on January 15, 2006.

Covers issues and advocacy relating to freedom and privacy in the online world.

Encyclopedia of Television. URL: http://www.museum.tv/archives/etv. Accessed on February 8, 2006.

An extensive online encyclopedia of the history of television, including technological developments, programming, and personalities.

I Want Media. URL: http://iwantmedia.com. Accessed on February 9, 2006.

Offers news and career links for media, both traditional and digital.

Library of American Broadcasting. URL: http://www.lib.umd.edu/LAB. Accessed on February 8, 2006.

Part of the University of Maryland library, this site offers a variety of reference guides and bibliographies relating to the history and development of broadcasting.

Pew/Internet. URL: http://www.pewinternet.org. Accessed on February 2, 2006.

Provides numerous in-depth reports on who is using the World Wide Web and Internet, popular applications, and changing trends.

Smithsonian Institution. Science and Technology Division, Computers and Communications Section. URL: http://www.si.edu/science_and_technology/computers_and_communications. Accessed on February 9, 2006.

Includes pages for a variety of exhibits, including "Information Age: People, Information & Technology."

TV Week. URL: http://www.tvweek.com. Accessed on February 9, 2006.

Gives the latest news from the television industry.

Webopedia. URL: http://www.webopedia.com. Accessed on February 8, 2006.

An online dictionary and encyclopedia of computer and Internet technology.

Periodicals

Advertising Age
Published by Crain Communications
711 Third Avenue
New York, NY 10017-4036
Telephone: (212) 210-0100

Premier publication about advertising trends, campaigns, and the advertising profession

Historical Journal of Film, Radio & Television
Published by the International Association for Media and History
Box 1216
Washington, CT 06793
Telephone: (213) 740-8005

Internet Week
Published by CMP Media
600 Community Drive
Manhasset, NY 11030
Telephone: (516) 562-5000

Weekly news about the business and technology of the Internet

Journal of Broadcasting & Electronic Media
Published by the Broadcast Educational Association
Editor: Donald G. Godfrey

Walter Cronkite School of Journalism and Mass Communications
Arizona State University
P.O. Box 871305
Telephone: (480) 965-8661
  Academic journal discussing trends in broadcasting and electronic media

PC Magazine
Published by Ziff-Davis Corporation
P.O. Box 54070
Boulder, CO 80322-4070
Telephone: (212) 503-3500
  Popular bimonthly magazine covering all aspects of PCs and other digital information and communications technologies

PC World
Published by IDG Data Group
501 Second Street
San Francisco, CA 94107
Telephone: (415) 243-0500
  Another popular magazine with wide coverage of computer technology from a consumer perspective

Technology Review
Published by the Massachusetts Institute of Technology
One Main Street
7th Floor
Cambridge, MA 02142
Telephone: (617) 475-8000
  Has in-depth features on leading-edge technologies, including computing and media

Wired
Published by Conde Nast
520 Third Street
Suite 305
San Francisco, CA 94107-1815
Telephone: (415) 276-5000

A colorful and provocative magazine on the Internet and cyberculture trends. Operates the HotWired.com Web site

Societies and Organizations

Association for Computing Machinery
http://www.acm.org
One Astor Plaza 1515 Broadway, 17th Floor
New York, NY 10036-5701
Telephone: (212) 869-7440

Association for Multimedia Communication
http://www.amcomm.org
P.O. Box 10645
Chicago, IL 60610
Telephone: (312) 409-1032

Center for Democracy and Technology
http://www.cddt.org
1634 I Street NW
Washington, DC 20006
Telephone: (202) 637-9800

Computer History Museum
http://www.computerhistory.org
1401 North Shoreline Boulevard
Mountain View, CA 94043
Telephone: (650) 810-1010

Electronic Frontier Foundation
http://www.eff.org
454 Shotwell Street
San Franciso, CA 94110-1914
Telephone: (415) 436-9333

Electronic Privacy Information Center
http://www.epic.org
1718 Connecticut Avenue NW, Suite 200

Washington, DC 20009
Telephone: (202) 483-1140

Information Technology Association of America
http://www.comptia.org
1815 South Meyers Road, Suite 300
Oakbrook Terrace, IL 60181-5228
Telephone: (630) 268-1818

Institute for Electrical and
Electronic Engineering Computer Society
http://www.computer.org
1730 Massachusetts Avenue NW
Washington, DC 20036-1992
Telephone: (202) 371-0101

Internet Society
http://www.isoc.org
12020 Sunrise Valley Drive, Suite 210
Reston, VA 20191-3429
Telephone: (703) 648-9888

MIT (Massachusetts Institute of Technology) Media Lab
http://www.media.mit.edu
Building E15 77
Massachusetts Avenue
Cambridge, MA 02139-4307
Telephone: (617) 253-5960

National Association of Broadcasters
http://www.nab.org
1771 N Street NW
Washington, DC 20036
Telephone: (202) 429-5300

Poynter Institute
http://www.poynter.org
801 Third Street South

St. Petersburg, FL 33701
Telephone: (888) 769-8387

Tech Museum of Innovation
http://www.thetech.org
201 South Market Street
San Jose, CA 95113
Telephone: (408) 294-TECH

World Wide Web Consortium
http://www.w3.org
Massachusetts Institute of Technology
32 Vassar Street, Room 32-G515
Cambridge, MA 02139
Telephone: (617) 253-2613

INDEX

191